A Relation, or Journal, of a Late Expedition, &c.

LIBRARY PRESS @UF

AN IMPRINT OF UF PRESS AND
GEORGE A. SMATHERS LIBRARIES

A Relation, or Journal, of a Late Expedition, &c.

EDWARD KIMBER

LibraryPress@UF

GAINESVILLE, FLORIDA

ISBN 978-1-947372-13-9 (pbk.)
ISBN 978-1-947372-16-0 (ePub)

LibraryPress@UF is an imprint of the University of Florida Press.

LIBRARY PRESS @ UF

AN IMPRINT OF UF PRESS AND
GEORGE A. SMATHERS LIBRARIES

University of Florida Press
15 Northwest 15th Street
Gainesville, FL 32611-2079
http://upress.ufl.edu

The Florida and the Caribbean Open Books Series

In 2016, the University Press of Florida, in collaboration with the George A. Smathers Libraries of the University of Florida, received a grant from the National Endowment for the Humanities and the Andrew W. Mellon Foundation, under the Humanities Open Books program, to republish books related to Florida and the Caribbean and to make them freely available through an open access platform. The resulting list of books is the Florida and the Caribbean Open Books Series published by the LibraryPress@UF in collaboration with the University of Florida Press, an imprint of the University Press of Florida. A panel of distinguished scholars has selected the series titles from the UPF list, identified as essential reading for scholars and students.

The series is composed of titles that showcase a long, distinguished history of publishing works of Latin American and Caribbean scholarship that connect through generations and places. The breadth and depth of the list demonstrates Florida's commitment to transnational history and regional studies. Selected reprints include Daniel Brinton's *A Guide-Book of Florida and the South* (1869), Cornelis Goslinga's *The Dutch in the Caribbean and on the Wild Coast, 1580–1680* (1972), and Nelson Blake's *Land into Water—Water into Land* (1980). Also of note are titles from the Bicentennial Floridiana Facsimile Series. The series, published in 1976 in commemoration of America's bicentenary, comprises twenty-five books regarded as "classics," out-of-print works that needed to be in more libraries and readers' bookcases, including Sidney Lanier's *Florida: Its Scenery, Climate, and History* (1875) and Silvia Sunshine's *Petals Plucked from Sunny Climes* (1880).

Today's readers will benefit from having free and open access to these works, as they provide unique perspectives on the historical scholarship on Florida and the Caribbean and serve as a foundation upon which today's researchers can build.

Visit LibraryPress@UF and the Florida and the Caribbean Open Books Series at http://ufdc.ufl.edu/librarypress.

Florida and the Caribbean Open Books Series Project Members

This book is reissued as part of the Humanities Open Books program, funded by a grant from the National Endowment for the Humanities and the Andrew W. Mellon Foundation.

Mary L. Singleton, Jacksonville
Bruce A. Smathers, Tallahassee
Alan Trask, Fort Meade
Edward J. Trombetta, Tallahassee
Ralph D. Turlington, Tallahassee
William S. Turnbull, Orlando
Robert Williams, Tallahassee
Lori Wilson, Merritt Island

GENERAL EDITOR'S PREFACE.

THE War of Jenkins' Ear which erupted in 1739 pitted Britain against Spain, and one of the prizes was Spanish Florida. The war received its whimsical name from an English smuggler, Robert Jenkins, who was captured years earlier off the Florida coast and whose ears were cut off by his Spanish captors. When he displayed these remarkably preserved pieces of his anatomy to the members of Parliament, they were outraged at this shameless Spanish atrocity. It so inflamed British public opinion that war seemed the only way to revenge the effrontery, restore the national pride, and at the same time expand Britain's empire in North America.

The war gave General James Edward Oglethorpe, British governor of Georgia, the opportunity that he had been seeking. When Spaniards raided Amelia Island and killed two Georgians, the general gathered his forces and marched into Florida, ravishing the countryside that he passed through. During the winter of 1740, he collected 900 British troops and nearly 1,000 Indians for an attack on the Spanish garrison in St. Augustine. Oglethorpe had no difficulty taking Fort St. George on the St. Johns River, and Forts Diego and Mosa quickly capitulated. St. Augustine was another matter. The Spanish were secure behind the thick coquina walls of the Castillo de San Marcos, and the British did not receive the support that they had expected from Carolina. In a letter written June 16, 1740 to Lieutenant Governor Bull of South Carolina, Oglethorpe noted: "We cannot besiege the Town by Land and Water with so small a force." With the approach of the hurricane season, the British, in July, 1740, withdrew their forces to Savannah. Once more, St. Augustine had stood firm against an adversary.

It was now Spain's turn to draw blood. Privateers plied up and down the coast, thirty English prizes were taken to St. Augustine, and plantations in Carolina and Georgia were plundered. In the summer of 1742, the Spanish took the offensive under the command of Governor Manuel de Montiano. The plan was to move by land and sea against Georgia and to avenge the assault against St. Augustine by "sacking and burning all the towns, posts, plantations, and settlements of the enemy." Oglethorpe, in the meantime, was strengthening his line of fortifications stretching southward from Frederica. He repaired old batteries, erected new ones, and improved the intricate system of interlocking communications. He was as prepared as possible when a large Spanish flotilla appeared off St. Simon Island on July 4, 1742. There were 2,000 in the invasion force, the largest ever to appear in that area. Oglethorpe had fewer than 700 men to defend Frederica. Undaunted, he displayed capable military leader-

ship, and in the battle which became known as
Bloody Marsh, he completely routed the Spanish.
Fearing the worst, Montiano hastily re-embarked
and returned to St. Augustine. The Spanish had
lost a golden opportunity to thwart the enemy.

The next year the Spanish made a hostile over-
land demonstration toward the St. Johns River,
but Oglethorpe rushed southward with part of
his regiment, with reinforcements from Virginia,
and with a contingent of Indian allies. The Spaniards were driven back behind the walls of St.
Augustine. Oglethorpe used many wiles, but he
was unable to lure his opponents into the open,
and once again frustrated, he returned to Frederica. Thus ended the dream of the British that
they could acquire Florida by military conquest.
In July, 1743 Oglethorpe returned to England,
saying farewell to the colony he had founded.
Two short decades later, in 1763, England would
acquire Florida through the political arrange-
ments included in the Treaty of Paris. What
seemed impossible on the battlefield was accom-
plished around the diplomatic table. After years
of turmoil and bitter skirmishing, the Union Jack
was unfurled over Florida, now a part of England's North American empire.

The bloody conflicts of the eighteenth century
involved Europe's great powers—Britain, Spain,
France, Prussia, and the Austro-Hungarian empire. The overseas colonies of these countries,
like British Georgia and Spanish Florida, were
but insignificant pawns in an international chess
game. The decisions which affected the lives and
futures of the settlers on the American frontier
were made thousands of miles away. The conflict
which pitted Florida and Georgia against each
other in the 1740s has not been extensively stud-

ied or chronicled by either American or European historians. One of the few accounts is by Edward Kimber who arrived in Georgia, January 7, 1743, and spent the next fifteen months in the service of General Oglethorpe. He was a member of the force which made the assault on St. Augustine, and his eyewitness account was published under the title, *A Relation, or Journal, of a Late Expedition to the Gates of St. Augustine, on Florida*. As Professor John TePaske of Duke University points out in his introduction to the facsimile edition of Kimber's report, the *"Relation* speaks for itself and needs few comments." It is the story of the raid written by a participant, and it supplies detailed information which is nowhere else available. Besides the *Relation*, Professor TePaske has also included in his introduction the letter written by Governor Montiano to the Spanish minister of marine and the Indies, José del Campillo. In it Montiano gave his version of the British attack and the Spanish defense.

John Jay TePaske is a graduate of Michigan State University and of Duke University. A recipient of a Ford Foundation Fellowship at the University of California, Berkeley, in 1962–1963, he has served as visiting professor at the University of Washington and the University of Texas. A member of the history faculty at Duke University, he is the author of *The Governorship of Spanish Florida* and the editor of *Three American Empires, The Character of Phillip II: The Problem of Moral Judgments in History*, and *Explosive Forces in Latin America*. The paper that he presented at the First Annual Florida Bicentennial Symposium at the University of Florida in 1972 is included in the volume, *Eighteenth-Century Florida and Its Borderlands* (Gainesville,

1975). Professor TePaske's articles have appeared in scholarly and professional journals in the United States and Mexico.

Edward Kimber's *Relation* is one of the twenty-five facsimile volumes of rare, out-of-print Florida history in the Bicentennial Floridiana Facsimile Series. It is being published by the Florida Bicentennial Commission as one of its major Bicentennial projects. The titles in the series were selected to represent the full spectrum of Florida's rich and exciting 450-year history. Scholars like Professor TePaske, with a special interest in and knowledge of Florida history, were invited to edit each volume, write an introduction, and compile an index. The goal of the Florida Bicentennial Commission in publishing the facsimile series is to make a lasting contribution to the scholarship of Florida and American history.

SAMUEL PROCTOR
General Editor of the
BICENTENNIAL FLORIDIANA
FACSIMILE SERIES

University of Florida

INTRODUCTION.

THE Southeast was for more than three centuries the center of a bitter contest for empire in North America. From Ponce de León's discovery of Florida in 1513 to its acquisition by the United States in 1821, England, France, Spain, and ultimately the United States contended with one another for control over the area. To 1670 the Spaniards prevailed. After several failures to establish a foothold in Florida early in the sixteenth century, the Spanish rose to a French challenge. In 1565 they established a permanent settlement at St. Augustine, destroyed the three-year-old Huguenot outpost at Fort Caroline on the St. Johns River, and annihilated the remnants of the French force at Matanzas Inlet south of St. Augustine at the same time.[1] Two and one-half years later Dominique de Gourgues got revenge for the events of 1565 when he terrorized the new Spanish settlement, but that was his only accomplishment. He could not prevent the expansion of the Spanish colonial effort in the Southeast. Relying on a vanguard of Franciscan missionaries and a few soldiers, the Spaniards extended their control over most of present-day Alabama, Florida, and Georgia. By the middle of the seventeenth century, the Franciscans boasted 26,000 converts among the Indians of the area.[2]

In 1670 the founding of Carolina by the English opened a new chapter in the struggle for empire. With lavish gifts of rum, guns, and other merchandise, the English began eroding the missionaries' influence over the Indians and destroying the chain of Franciscan outposts which had served as the bulwarks of Spanish control. By 1700, in fact, the Carolinians and their Indians had effectively reduced Spanish control over the natives to a few small villages around St. Augustine and Apalache. During Queen Anne's War the English scourged Florida. In 1702 they almost destroyed St. Augustine, and in 1704 they swept through Apalache to the west near the Gulf Coast, forcing the evacuation and destruction of Fort San Luis. Border raids by Carolinians, Spaniards, and their Indian allies grew more frequent and more bitter. Even after Queen Anne's War ended in 1713, the frontier was continuously restive as England continued her relentless expansion south from Charleston.[3]

Still another threat to the Spanish in Florida came in 1732 with James Oglethorpe's settlement of Georgia. Adept at gaining Indian allies, Oglethorpe inspired Indian raids on Spanish Florida. In 1740 during the War of Jenkins' Ear the Georgia governor mounted a massive siege of St. Augustine, but as in the attack of 1702, the English failed to shake the Spanish from their position on the Bahama Channel. Indecision, bungling, and lack of coordination by the English, a daring middle-of-the-night raid by the Spanish on Ogle-

thorpe's positions north of the town, and timely
relief from Cuba forced the English to give up
their assault.[4]

Oglethorpe's siege led to Spanish reprisals. In
1742, the governor of Florida, Manuel de Montiano, launched an all-out offensive against Fort
Frederica on St. Simon Island. In the end he was
no more successful than Oglethorpe at St. Augustine two years earlier. Unable to take advantage
of superior numbers of men, ships, and arms,
Montiano proved indecisive and diffident, particularly after an English victory at Bloody Marsh
south of Frederica in July, 1742. Like Oglethorpe,
he had to retreat and make excuses for his failure
to his angry superiors in Havana and Madrid.
Almost immediately, in September, 1742, Oglethorpe counterattacked, but a storm broke up the
English fleet anchored off the bar of St. Augustine, and the Georgians retired.[5] But they returned again in March, 1743, in the raid described
by Edward Kimber in *A Relation, or Journal, of
a Late Expedition to the Gates of Saint Augustine, on Florida.*

Edward Kimber, 1719–1769.

Edward Kimber, says one biographer gratui-
tously, did nothing more in life than eke out "a
scanty subsistence by compiling for booksellers,
and died, worn out with such drudgery, in
1769."[6] Kimber might well have retained this reputation for posterity; but his great-great-grand-
son Sidney A. Kimber, a curious Georgia bib-
liophile Leonard L. Mackall, and a Harvard
litterateur Frank Gees Black have rescued him
from this pitiful epitaph.[7] That he was something

of a drudge cannot be denied: he was an expert corrector, editor, genealogist, compiler, and indexer. He was also, however, a soldier, journalist, novelist, and poet of considerable talent and imagination.

Edward Kimber was greatly influenced by his father Isaac, a man of modest reputation in London literary circles. Born in Berkshire in December, 1692, Isaac received an excellent education, first studying language under a John Ward at Gresham College and then taking work in philosophy and divinity to qualify for the Baptist ministry.[8] That his grandfather on his mother's side was a Baptist divine may well have led him into this calling.[9] Isaac was a failure in the ministry, lasting only six years. His first parish was in London, Paul's Alley, Barbican, and there he earned a reputation as a dull preacher—he read his sermons. In June, 1724, after two years in London, Isaac became assistant pastor in a Baptist church in Nantwich, Cheshire. Three years later he returned to London to take a post as assistant minister of two small parishes. When the two united the following year, he voluntarily or unwillingly gave up the active ministry, but whatever the reason, he simply was not suited for preaching and parish work.[10]

Isaac Kimber's first secular venture was the editing of a new periodical, *The Monthly Chronicle*, to compete with the widely read *Gentleman's Magazine*. He was a good choice as editor and well fitted for the task because in order to supplement his meager parson's salary, he had for several years corrected for various London printers and editors. *The Monthly Chronicle* lasted more than four years (January, 1728, to May, 1732), and after it suspended publication,

Isaac became editor of the more prestigious *London Magazine*, a post he held until his death in 1755.[11] Besides editing, he was involved in a number of other cultural endeavors. He wrote history and biography, supervised compilation of a Latin dictionary, and for a time took over a school formerly run by his old professor, John Ward.[12] Isaac had at least two sons—Edward and Richard—who were both close to their father. They may have been so close because of the need to care for Isaac's wife and their mother, who went insane and remained a trial to the family for over twenty years.[13]

Of Edward Kimber's youth and education little is known. Born in 1719, he grew up among his father's dissatisfied Baptist parishioners and the literati who wrote for *The Monthly Chronicle* and *The London Magazine*. Except for primary school, Edward was educated by his father, a learned and exacting tutor. As part of his education, Edward assisted in editing and writing for *The London Magazine*, contributing short poems, essays, obituaries, and the like. That Isaac and his son Edward wrote so much themselves may have been caused by the more prestigious *Gentleman's Magazine*'s having a corner on the services of the better known writers. Also *The London Magazine* may not have had the money to pay its authors.[14]

At twenty-three Edward Kimber left England for America. Why he made the journey is not clear, but probably he had enlisted in Oglethorpe's service. At the same time he may have been seeking wider experiences on which to draw later for his novels and essays. Whatever the reason, he left Gravesend for New York in the fall of 1742, arriving some six weeks later, on November 1. Resting for two weeks in New York, he sailed on the sloop *Newbould* for Maryland and Virginia. At Yorktown two days before Christmas he boarded another vessel, the *Bradley Lucas*, which arrived in Georgia January 7, 1743. Here Kimber spent the next fifteen months in the service of Governor Oglethorpe.[15]

Jottings in his diary, articles published later in *The London Magazine*, and the *Relation* provide at least some clues to his activities in America. Almost immediately after his arrival in Georgia, he joined Oglethorpe's band of soldiers and Indians for the assault on St. Augustine, which he details in the *Relation*. Upon his return to Frederica, he evidently remained in military service (there are no entries in his diary from January, 1743, to March 23, 1744) and traveled about the colony. He went to Savannah and also visited an orphanage run by George Whitfield, the revivalist preacher of the Great Awakening. Predisposed to think of Whitfield as bigoted and uncharitable, Kimber changed his mind when he observed conditions at the orphanage where he found the forty young people of both sexes neatly dressed and well fed. Whitfield, Kimber observed, inculcated "Sobriety, Industry, and Frugality" among those in his charge.[16]

Edward left Georgia in late March, 1744. Moving northward, he visited Beaufort and Port Royal Island and reached Charleston on April 10. Ten days later he embarked for England on *The Two Sisters*, which arrived at the Orkney Islands on June 9, and Leith, near Edinburgh, June 15. A week later Kimber sailed for Gravesend, finally reaching London and home in July, 1744.[17]

[xvii]

In America, Kimber wrote down his impressions, which were later published in *The London Magazine* in 1745 and 1746.[18] Based on his voyage from New York to Georgia and his return by way of Charleston, the articles appeared under various pseudonyms—Americus, Cimber, Cynicus, and Historicus—and provided valuable commentary on conditions at that time in the southern colonies. He described coastal Georgia: "The Marshes and Savannas extended along their Borders, dispos'd with so seeming a Regularity, as to make the whole prospect look like one continu'd Canal, the Effect of the most studious Contrivance: Whilst at a distant View you take in a large Tract of hoary Woods, interspers'd with verdant Spots that bear the Semblance of the most refreshing Meadows: rustick Grottos, rugged Caverns, mossy Caves, and cooling Cells, seem to border their Sides. Here the lofty Oak, with all his kindred Tribe, clad in robes of antique Moss, seems, by its venerable Appearance, to be the real Monarch of the Woods; the Cedar, sweet as the Cedar of *Lebanon*; the towering evergreen Pine, the fragrant Hickary, the mournful Cypress, and here and there the triumphant Laurel, are seen in full Lustre, and preside over an Infinity of lesser Products, that seem to venerate, beneath, their more advanc'd and distinguish'd Neighbors. The savory Sassafras Shrub perfumes the Air, the Prickly-Pear Shrub offers his tempting Fruit to the Hand, but wisely tells you, by the Points that guard it, not to indulge to Excess; the delicious Mulberry, the swelling Peach, the Olive, the Pomegranate, the Walnut, all combine to furnish out the Paradisaical Banquet."[19]

He was floridly eloquent in his descriptions of wildlife—deer, mockingbirds, larks, mullet, catfish, oysters, and the "dreadful Alligator." He was also acutely aware of the pesty insects. Mosquitoes had the bite of a rattlesnake and were to be suffered along with the sandflies, ticks, and cockroaches. Savannah impressed him as a healthful place. Here, unlike Charleston, rain water dried up quickly and left "no noxious Steams" to cause agues (10–13, 18).

He also described conditions in other southern colonies. In Maryland he observed that English factors had so severely abused tobacco farmers that they were shifting from tobacco to grain and livestock production for export to the West Indies (35). In Maryland, Virginia, and the Carolinas he was astonished at the number of "Colonels, Majors, and Captains" he encountered; militia officers were so numerous that the colonies seemed a "Retreat for Heroes." But his astonishment turned to disgust when he saw these men at muster. They were unsightly, unkempt in their diverse uniforms, and undisciplined. In fact, he claimed that their appearance would nauseate him forever after at the sight of a sword or military sash (36). On slavery Kimber was adamant. "Thou worst and greatest of Evils," he wrote, "I view thee in the Semblance of a Wretch trod upon by ermin'd and turban'd Tyrants, and with poignant, heartbreaking Sighs, dragging after thee a toilsome Length of Chain, or bearing *African* burdens" (40).

Kimber was very impressed by Virginia, the most opulent of the colonies he visited. For his palate he found excellent wines, brandies, and rum, even bottled English port. Trade was brisk in Virginia, and her people consumed prodigious quantities of beef, pork, and grain. He was impressed too with the magnificence of the houses in Yorktown, and thought they were the equal of the best at Saint James. But he could not say the same for the coaches drawn by horses of varying colors. In one case he was appalled to see black, white, and chestnut horses in the same harness. Roads in Virginia were among the best he had ever seen, "infinitely superior to most in *England*" (59–60). Yorktown impressed him more than Williamsburg, "a most wretch'd contriv'd Affair for the Capital of a Country, being near Three Miles from the Sea in a bad Situation. There is nothing considerable in it, but the College, the Governor's House, and one or two more, which are no bad Piles." He termed William and Mary College a "Resort of all the Children, whose Parents can afford it" (60, 47). The students had excellent, cultured teachers, but the college was not equal to those in Massachusetts. Youth in the South, stated Kimber, were "pamper'd much more in Softness and Ease than their Neighbours more Northward" (48). Students did not study as hard nor were they as polite. He blamed this on parents who allowed their children "to consort with young Negroes, which insensibly causes them to imbibe their Manners and broken Speech" (48). Taverns were numerous "and much frequented" to taint the morals of the young. "Schemes of Gain, or Parties of Gaming and Pleasure, muddy too much their Souls and banish from amongst them the glorious Propensity to doing good" (60).

His return to England did not end Kimber's military career, and he continued periodic service at least until the end of 1748. In September, 1745, for example, he served for two weeks aboard

the *Success*, a warship of forty guns, relieving a
Captain George Dunbar. His command consisted
of four sergeants, three corporals, one drum, fifty-
nine privates, thirty-three women, and twelve
children. In all, he notes, between March 10,
1743, and December 4, 1748, he received almost
one hundred pounds for various periods of military or naval service.[20] Kimber also married after
his return from Georgia, probably in late 1744
or early 1745. His wife, Susanna Lunn Kimber,
bore him at least one son, George Thorpe Kimber, but otherwise little is known of his personal
life.[21]

Besides occasional periods of military service,
Kimber continued to write, compile, and edit. He
also obtained a modest reputation for eight novels, published between 1750 and 1765.[22] They all
followed the same pattern. Each was written in
the first person as fictionalized autobiography,
purportedly based on the author's papers or
diary. All the novels were anonymous. All of
Kimber's heroes were patterned more or less on
Henry Fielding's *Tom Jones*, with outlandishly
coincidental encounters, narrow escapes, hilari-
ous amorous adventures, mistaken identities, and
bawdy characters. Some drew heavily from Kimber's American experiences, particularly *The Life
and Adventures of Joe Thompson* and *The History of the Life and Adventures of Mr. Anderson.*
That they were eminently readable for English-
men of the mid-eighteenth century is clear from
the number of editions published. *Joe Thompson*
went through six English printings; *Mr. Anderson*, six; *James Ramble*, two; *David Ranger*,
three; *Neville Frowde*, three; *The Happy Orphans*, three; *Maria*, four; and *William Goldsmith*, three. Kimber's books were also read in

Europe. *Joe Thompson* was published in Paris, Frankfurt, and Leipzig; and *William Goldsmith* appeared in French translation.[23]

In his time Kimber was considered little better than a third-rate novelist. He wrote far too rapidly and insisted upon following the pattern of his first novel, *Joe Thompson*. He thrived on the melodramatic; and morality, justice, and goodness always triumphed for his heroes after severe challenges from immorality, injustice, and evil. One modern observer, however, finds some redeeming qualities in Kimber's books. For the social historian, he states, Kimber's descriptions of colonial America, life in a Fleet Street prison, and English tradesmen are excellent. Perhaps too, says this critic, if Kimber had taken more time to learn the art of the novel and had not been diverted by his compiling and editing, he might have improved his technique and at least approached second-rate status. Above all, however, Kimber's novels redeem him from his reputation as a drudge. He obviously had a lively imagination, keen sense of humor, an eye for the ridiculous, and a romantic sensibility.[24]

What were the other activities that kept him from being a good novelist? He wrote for *The London Magazine*—poetry, essays, travel accounts, obituaries, and similar items—and he assisted in the editing. For these jobs he earned one pound a week. He also compiled indices for the periodical in 1752, 1753, and 1754, pocketing three pounds each for these endeavors. Then, in 1755, when his father died, Edward became editor, serving in this capacity until his death in 1769.[25] Kimber engaged in a host of other activities, some of little consequence. He prepared lists of fairs with dates for England and Wales, compiled almanacs, wrote a handbook for gardeners, rendered advice to fishermen in an angler's magazine, drew up a guide for women letter writers, edited parliamentary debates for publication, and worked on lists of the English peerage.[26] Whether he made a meager living at such tasks or was well paid is not clear, but he was not poor. Kimber obviously had the discipline and the knack for his Grub Street endeavors —compiling indexes, garnering genealogical information, correcting the copy of others, and making concordances. Thus his reputation as a drudge. Yet viewing his whole career, one sees another side to Edward Kimber, a man with a multiplicity of interests, who was energetic, creative, and vital. That he died in 1769 worn out with the drudgery of compiling and correcting may have been partially true, but Kimber's other achievements belie this epitaph.

The Raid on St. Augustine.

Kimber's *Relation* speaks for itself and needs few comments. Published in 1744 under a pseudonym (G. L. Campbell, v. E. K.), it appeared in the form of a letter written to the Reverend Mr. Isaac K——r in London. In many respects it resembles Kimber's later novels, especially in its anonymity and narration in the first person. In its style the *Relation* is very much like the "Observations" on America which appeared later in *The London Magazine*, both flowery and effusive. In the main, however, Kimber narrates the course of events from February 26 to March 31, 1743, as a participant in the Florida expedition. Only at the end when he eulogizes Oglethorpe's courage and greatness does he deviate from straight-forward narration of this small episode in the inter-colonial struggle in the Southeast.[27] Still, despite the fact the *Relation* speaks for itself, it can be understood far better against the back-drop of events unfolding in Georgia and Florida during the War of Jenkins' Ear.

When Oglethorpe first came to Georgia in 1732, he was discreet in his relations with his Spanish neighbors. While wooing Indian allies with rum, guns, and presents, he was cautious at first not to incite them against the Spanish. He knew that Indian raids on Spain's settlements in Florida would only inspire retaliatory attacks on his own infant colony, and he tried to restrain the Carolinians from antagonizing the Indians against the Spaniards, lest he have to bear the brunt of an assault by the vengeful Floridians.[28] By 1738, however, he felt secure enough to become more aggressive, and less constrained about inhibiting his Indian allies. During the summer of that year, Lower Creeks raided Spanish settlements around St. Augustine and moved up the St. Johns River to the twin forts of Pupo and Picolata west of St. Augustine. Here the Creeks ravaged the stock-ades and killed two soldiers.[29] Uchizes under Oglethorpe's urging followed soon after, blocking the trail between St. Augustine and Apalache and investing Spanish Indian villages west of the pre-sidio of Fort San Marcos.[30] A counterattack by Spanish Indians on Amelia Island in November, 1739, resulted in the killing and mangling of two unfortunate English woodcutters but accom-plished little else.[31]

With the outbreak of the War of Jenkins' Ear in the Southeast, these border skirmishes gave way to more extensive fighting. In January, 1740,

Oglethorpe sent a force of two hundred Creek, Chickasaw, and Uchize warriors and a few Highland Rangers up the St. Johns, again to Pupo and Picolata. Here the Highlanders and Indians killed twelve infantrymen before they sent the Spanish garrisons of the two blockhouses scurrying back to St. Augustine.[32] With this as his prelude, the Georgia governor launched a major invasion in the late spring of 1740. With over sixteen hundred men, seven warships, and forty small dugouts, he aimed to oust the Spanish from Florida once and for all. The story of that attack has been well told elsewhere,[33] but in the end Oglethorpe failed. Although his siege of St. Augustine lasted less than a month (June 13 to July 4, 1740), his inability to coordinate his troops and naval forces, the impregnability of Fort San Marcos, a surprise Spanish attack on English positions north of St. Augustine, and relief ships from Cuba all combined to frustrate the Georgian's attempt to take Florida. Edward Kimber put the blame elsewhere: Oglethorpe, he wrote, "was betray'd and neglect'd by the mean *Carolina* Regiment, and many of the Men of War."[34]

In the summer of 1742 the Spaniards took their turn at all-out offensive. Under Governor Manuel de Montiano, they brought together a force of nineteen hundred men, five large men-of-war, and forty-nine small boats, all intended for an assault on Fort Frederica, focal point of English power in Georgia. As had Oglethorpe in Florida two years earlier, Montiano failed. His invasion attempt in June and July, 1742 was frustrated by his own timidity, bad weather, lack of familiarity with the terrain, a decisive English victory at Bloody Marsh south of Frederica, and lack of supplies. In the end Montiano's only accomplishments were the burning of two English blockhouses on Cumberland Island and some fields on St. Simon and Jekyll islands. In Spain José del Campillo, Minister of Marine and the Indies, was furious and railed against Montiano's "poor leadership, lack of diligence, and inefficiency."[85]

Thus, in 1740 and 1742 the English and Spanish had each launched a major offensive. Both had failed, and with Montiano's defeat at Bloody Marsh, the complexion of the war in the Southeast changed. Hostilities turned into small raids and counterraids by tiny bands of whites and Indians on each side, and marked an end to costly large expeditions. The failures of 1740 and 1742 and subsequent events have led one observer to state that the struggle in the Southeast in the wars of the 1740s consisted of "a great deal of grandiloquent marchings back and forth, much mismanagement, bad luck, and disappointment on the part of both sides, so much as to make it appear at times like a comic opera."[86] That it seemed farcical for contemporaries is clear from the comments of one disillusioned Boston rhymester:

From Georgia to Augustine the General goes;
From Augustine to Georgia come our foes;
Hardy from Charleston to St. Simon hies,
Again from there to Charleston back he flies.
Forth from St. Simons then the Spaniards
    creep;
'Say Children, Is not this your Bo Peep'?[87]

The Raid from English Sources.

For Oglethorpe the raid on St. Augustine in 1743, which Edward Kimber described in the *Relation*, was an attempt to retaliate for the Spanish

assault on Frederica in July, 1742, but more immediately, to avenge the Yamasee raid on the
trading post, Mount Venture, on the Altamaha
in November, 1742. In the latter attack Yamasees
had burned the main house at Mount Venture
and had taken five prisoners—four rangers and an
Indian servant. Compassionately they had left
the commandant's wife and her young baby behind. But on the way south, on some provocation,
the Yamasees suddenly killed two of the prisoners, turned back to the trading post, and murdered the mother and her infant daughter. On
the return trek to St. Augustine, however, the
Indian servant escaped and notified Oglethorpe
of what had happened. The Indian reported—
and rumors were rampant in both St. Augustine
and Frederica—that the Spaniards were girding
for another major offensive against Georgia. Oglethorpe responded by sending Captain John Williams and Lieutenant Colonel Alexander Heron
north to Carolina, Virginia, and Maryland to seek
recruits. Williams ultimately returned with 30
cavalrymen, Heron with 211 infantrymen, Edward Kimber among them.[38]

Besides these new recruits Oglethorpe received
aid from the Lower Creeks and their chief, Chi-
gilly. Previously these Indians had been reluctant
to join the English in attacks on Spanish settlements; now they were eager for revenge on the
Yamasees for their destruction of the trading post
at Mount Venture, which had been so useful to
them.[39] By the end of February Oglethorpe had
assembled a detachment of 200 of his own regu-
lars, the 211 soldiers recruited by Heron, the 30
cavalrymen, some Scotch Highlanders, a few
sailors, and 80 (70?) Lower Creek warriors. To
transport this force, he procured the guard

schooner, *Walker*, and two private schooners, *The Sea Flower* and *Elizabeth*. Although not a large enough force to oust the Spaniards from St. Augustine, Oglethorpe believed it capable of blocking at last the incursions of the Spaniards and their Indian allies on Georgia.[40]

The expedition departed Frederica on Sunday, February 27, to the thunder of a twenty-one-gun salute. Those not embarking on the larger ocean-going vessels made their way south in the small scout boats and piraguas, following the inland waterway south toward the St. Johns. On March 3 and 4 Oglethorpe ordered his men to disembark on Amelia and Cumberland islands for a respite, while he continued with an advance party. On the south bank of the St. Johns he established a base camp and sent word back to his men at Fort Prince William to join him. At the same time he obtained additional naval support from the yawl *Success*, commanded by a Captain William Thomson, who reported also that he had encountered two large warships out of Jamaica, the *Kent* and the *York*, with seventy and sixty guns respectively. They were in the area hoping to seize the galleon and small ship bound from Havana to St. Augustine with supplies and money for the Florida garrison.[41]

By March 9 all of Oglethorpe's troops had gathered at his camp on the St. Johns to prepare for the assault on St. Augustine. Meanwhile, the eighty Creek warriors moved toward the presidio to reconnoiter the area, where they hoped to capture a live prisoner to provide Oglethorpe with information on the strength of the Spanish garrison. Advancing to the western bank of the Diego River near Fort San Marcos, the warrior band ambushed a Spanish longboat filled with a troop of twenty men and two officers who were escorting a band of forced laborers digging sod to shore up the hornworks of the fort. In the ambush the Indians killed one soldier and five of the forced laborers; one officer, eleven soldiers, and six laborers were wounded. The two soldiers taken prisoner were mutilated and then scalped in retaliation for the one Indian killed by a Spanish musket. Although the skirmish had occurred close enough for Montiano to hear the musket fire, he could not retaliate; he lacked the piraguas needed to cross the Diego River. The next day, however, he dispatched a search party, but the cavalry force found nothing. The Indians had retired north after the ambush.[42]

The Indians reached Oglethorpe's encampment on the St. Johns on March 11 and presented the governor with five scalps, a severed hand, and a number of severed arms. They claimed that they had killed over forty Spaniards. In return for these macabre gifts, Oglethorpe proffered wine and food, and then invited them to join him in his projected attack on St. Augustine. All but four refused and left the English camp for their villages to the north.[43]

Undeterred by the defection of the seventy-five Lower Creeks, Oglethorpe went ahead with his plans. His strategy called for his forces to march close to St. Augustine, to send a few soldiers and Indians under the guns of the presidio as bait to lure Montiano's cavalry footsoldiers out of the sanctuary of Fort San Marcos, and finally to ambush and defeat them, much as he had done at Bloody Marsh in 1742. He knew that one reason for his failure in 1740 was the Spaniards' refusal to come out and fight. Now he hoped to entice them into open country where he and his forces would have the advantage. Leaving their camp on the St. Johns on March 14, the English forces marched south along the Atlantic beach, spending their first night on the dunes along the coast. The next morning they moved inland, heading southwest along an old trail to deserted Fort San Diego. By the following day they reached a site called the Grove, about five miles northwest of St. Augustine, where they stopped briefly to rest and quench their thirst. Pressing on, they advanced to within three miles of the presidio, but at this juncture Oglethorpe suddenly was forced to change his plans. One of his men had deserted to the Spaniards, eliminating the element of surprise and causing Oglethorpe to order a forced march northward where he could refashion his plans without endangering his men.[44]

On the hard march north Oglethorpe had another inspiration. He believed that once the deserter poured out information on the strength and position of the English troops, Montiano would come out in force to attack. Thus, on March 17 he ordered his sleepless, insect-ridden men to prepare another ambush for the expected Spanish assault. But the Spaniards never materialized. Montiano preferred to stay within the friendly confines of Fort San Marcos. Frustrated and outraged, Oglethorpe tried to force the Spaniards into the ambush. With six rangers he rode to the very walls of San Marcos, but this only caused several terrified sentries to rush inside the presidio. Montiano was evidently willing to let Oglethorpe's force roam the area unmolested and unchallenged.[45]

With no one to fight, yet not strong enough to besiege San Marcos, Oglethorpe was in a quandary. His way out was a decision to remain in the area three more days, hoping that Montiano would ultimately make a move. Returning to his main force, he ordered his men to remain at their positions ready to meet a Spanish attack. Again, the desertion of one of his men forced a change in his plans, and on March 18 he called for an immediate retreat lest his forces be caught in a trap, and then they broke camp and headed back to the St. Johns.[46]

Oglethorpe was probably wise to retire, since the deserter provided Montiano with precise information on both the size and strength of the English expedition. He also exposed Oglethorpe's plan to take a live prisoner from whom he could extract information on Spanish forces in St. Augustine and destroy Montiano's cavalry in ambush. More than that, the deserter said that one hundred Caveta Indians would arrive in April to reinforce the main body of Oglethorpe's troops. Montiano also learned of the naval strength of the British expedition—the galiot at the bar of the St. Johns with fourteen guns of nine, six, and four-pounds caliber; the two piraguas with four cannon; several others with two and three; the six launches; and the two large men-of-war lying in wait for the subsidy and supply ships from Cuba.[47]

Although the retreat back to the St. Johns on March 18 marked the end of major land operations, it did not mean the termination of lesser ventures. On March 19, for example, Highlanders under Lieutenant Charles MacKay took a scout boat, the *Darien*, up the St. Johns to Fort Pupo to see if the blockhouse had been rebuilt and reinforced. At the same time twenty newly arrived Creeks went out in search of Spanish scalps near

St. Augustine, but when they approached the town, they closed with a band of Spanish Yamasees and were badly beaten. On March 25 still another band of fifty Cherokees, Upper Creeks, and Lower Creeks trekked south to get revenge on the Yamasee, but this time neither the Spanish Indians nor the Spaniards would come out to fight.[48]

Despite his frustrations on land, Oglethorpe was still eager to use his naval superiority. On March 21, for example, three vessels, including the British man-of-war *Rye* under Captain Charles Hardy, the galley *Charlestown* under a Captain Lightfoot, and the frigate *Success* under Captain William Thomson, anchored near Oglethorpe's command post on the St. Johns. In the conference which ensued the governor proposed that they singe the Spaniards' beards once more by invading Santa Anastasia Island. The Spaniards pastured their cattle on the island, and Oglethorpe saw the opportunity to cut off the meat supply for the town and presidio. The three ships could be used to cover the landing of his troops and take them off after they had slaughtered the cattle. Hardy refused to participate, but Thompson proved more cooperative and agreed to escort and cover the boats containing the eighty-man English and Indian invasion force. On March 28 they made their first attempt to land on the island, but the surf was too high, and they had to give up. Two subsequent attempts on March 29 and 30 failed for the same reason, forcing Oglethorpe once more to forsake his plans. Thus, with the forces still remaining in the area, he departed for home with little to show for his efforts.[49]

The Raid from Spanish Sources.

With some embellishment from Spanish sources, the foregoing constitutes a somewhat fuller version of what Edward Kimber saw as a participant in the English raid on St. Augustine in 1743. But the episode has another side as well, that of the timid Manuel de Montiano in Fort San Marcos, fending off Oglethorpe's thrust into Florida. For Montiano the attack of the Spanish Yamasees on Mount Venture late in November, 1742 was crucial. In his version of the raid he reported that Indians friendly to the Spaniards had assaulted the blockhouse on the Altamaha (he said the English name was Tamaja). Inside they found five English cavalrymen, one Indian, a woman, and her infant daughter. Three of the soldiers died during the initial fighting, leaving as prisoners two horsemen, the Indian, the wife of the commandant, and her child. After imbibing a vast quantity of wine, the Indians then burned the blockhouse and threw all the goods that they could not carry with them into the Altamaha River. With two English soldiers and the Indian as prisoners, they left Mount Venture for St. Augustine. The Indian, it appeared, was happy to be captured by the Spaniards and to leave English tutelage, but this was only a cover. After four days he escaped into the woods. The Yamasee had no idea where he had gone.[50]

When the Indians arrived at St. Augustine early in December, Montiano immediately interrogated the two cavalrymen. They reported that 1,000 troops were in Charleston awaiting the arrival of Admiral Edward Vernon, who would take them south to join James Oglethorpe for another siege of St. Augustine in the spring of

1743. Vernon would command the naval forces, Oglethorpe the land army. Where the 1,000 men in Charleston had come from was not clear to the English prisoners.[51] That the English intended a major offensive in 1743 was also confirmed by the commandant of Spanish Pensacola[52] and an Irish artilleryman serving in the Havana garrison who obtained his information from a British sailor from Providence.[53] (This is a good example of how rumors spread in mid-eighteenth-century Florida.) In fact these rumors had proved so compelling that the governor of Cuba, Francisco de Güemes y Horcasitas, sent three hundred troops to Florida under Lieutenant Colonel Juan Pichón and a large quantity of wheat, meat, vegetables, and other supplies.[54] Montiano reacted by fortifying the Matanzas Inlet with a permanent stone installation erected on the soft mud of the island commanding the entrance to the bar. At the presidio he worked feverishly to strengthen the earthworks around the inland approaches to Fort San Marcos.[55] In fact the party of soldiers and forced laborers surprised in the Creek ambush at the Diego River were digging sod for the hornworks of the fort.

This, then, was the situation in St. Augustine at the time Oglethorpe launched his attack in March, 1743. It is clear that both Montiano and the governor of Cuba expected a major siege, much like that of 1740. They did not know that Oglethorpe planned something less, and this may explain Montiano's reluctance to engage the Indians and English forces roaming so freely in the woods north of St. Augustine. Fortunately we also have a Spanish version of the events described by Edward Kimber. Montiano gave his side of the episode in a letter to the Spanish Minister of Marine and the Indies, José del Campillo:[56]

Sir:

In a letter of March 12 Your Excellency includes a written testimony of Don Domingo de la Cruz in which he shows his surprise at learning that the English in Carolina are preparing an expedition that he believes is aimed at this presidio. He also informs Your Excellency about the illegal contacts which resulted during the exchange of prisoners, despite a promise of Parliament to the contrary. He argues that when the same thing occurred here we zealously observed the agreement made between the two crowns, and this particular fact ought to obligate them to subscribe more closely to the agreement.[57] Now, I will say to Your Excellency how surprised I was on March 11th to see a frigate and two galiots passing in front of this presidio. Then, on the 21st a troop of eighty Indians friendly to the English surprised a detachment of twenty men, one sub-lieutenant, and a sergeant, who were protecting the forced laborers employed in digging up sod for the hornworks being erected for the greater security of this presidio. The Indians killed one soldier and five forced laborers; seriously wounded the officer, sergeant, eleven soldiers, and six forced laborers; and captured two soldiers, whom, according to the testimony of a deserter, they also murdered in a barbaric fashion. Unfortunately, despite their proximity to the fort, I could not come to the aid of this party, not only because of the suddenness of their assault but also because our piraguas were on the other side of the river and there was no way to ferry our troops across. The next day cavalrymen

went out to reconnoiter the area. They found a
trail and indications that a large number of men
had been there waiting in ambush, posted at the
only spot where a land detachment could have
come to the aid of our men if the Indians had
not retired as soon as they made their attack.
But God saved us from this trap whose effects
would have been so fatal and impossible to prevent at that moment.

The next day on the 22nd a frigate was seen
to the north, and subsequently another two, plying the waters near the coast on the 24th, 26th,
27th, and 28th.

On the 28th the deserter already cited entered
this presidio. He said that Oglethorpe had three
hundred men from his regiment in the vicinity,
that he had come with the object of taking a live
prisoner and destroying our cavalry. He knew
that our horsemen sally out whenever there is
some abnormal activity in the area and that they
often reconnoiter as far north as the St. Johns
River. To this end he brought thirty cavalrymen
and twenty-one Scotch Highlanders in addition
to the Indians. Moreover, the deserter believed
he [Oglethorpe] had another scheme as well: he
was waiting for one hundred Caveta Indians and
Colonel Cook who would arrive in April as reinforcements for his troop in order to lay siege to
this presidio.

When the deserter arrived at the St. Johns,
there was one galiot with fourteen guns of nine-,
six-, and four-pound caliber; one large piragua
with four guns; another with one four pounder;
some smaller vessels; and six long boats. The
captain of a frigate which crossed the bar, ad-
vised Oglethorpe that one vessel of sixty guns
and another of fifty, which they had not been

informed of before starting out, were in coastal waters close by, lying in wait for the ship which ought to bring the subsidy for the presidio.

The 29th and 30th the two frigates and the galiot stayed close in, and at dusk three other ships appeared, but their courses could not be determined.

With these vessels in the vicinity and trusting the deserter because he gave such a true, consistently clear picture of the strength of their forces, I did not take any action to counter Oglethorpe's audacious activities except on the 29th to send out a party of Indians, accompanied by two Spaniards, to reconnoiter their encampment and bring back news of what they saw. Upon their return to this presidio after five days, they informed me that Oglethorpe had penetrated into this area with the same number of men the deserter had given me. Accordingly, they inferred from the trail they left that they had retreated but only to the St. Johns where it was impossible to seize a sentry because their camp lay in the open with a great many men in the vicinity. Outside the mouth of the bar lay two frigates and a galiot, and inside the bar, the galiot and other piraguas and launches to which the deserter had already referred.

Upon their [the Spanish Indians] return here at ten in the evening of the 2nd, three leagues from this presidio, they encountered a group of enemy Indians headed toward the St. Johns. Once our Indians became aware of their presence, they lay in wait in ambush and successfully fired on them with light muskets. Our men really did not know how much damage they did. Although three enemy Indians lay dead and though the remainder of their force scurried into the

woods, our party did not want to stop to ferret
them out because they did not want to risk the
loss of any more men. Still, they believed the
enemy Indians were very badly battered since
they did not return our fire.

As a result of all that has been discussed so far,
I can finally inform Your Excellency what I have
been able to discover about the ships which have
just been seen near this place. There are three
frigates, four galiots, and two flatboats, which
have sailed off in different directions. Later on
the 8th one frigate, four galiots, and two flatboats
approached this bar and that of Matanzas. Be-
lieving they were going to attack that fort, I dispatched four galiots to stop them from entering
the mouth of the river. Because the English rec-
ognized the difficulty of their venture, or for some
other reason that cannot be explained, they retired on the 10th without having made an assault.

A large number of Indians remained in this
vicinity. I conjectured from what the deserter
said that they were waiting for General Oglethorpe and were there to join his regular troops.
Although their activities were not sufficient cause
for concern, I still could not ignore Oglethorpe's
overall design, especially if he were awaiting
additional aid that would enable him to carry
through his original plan. Thus, I maintained the
necessary vigilance, communicating everything
that occurred to the governor in Havana so that
with this knowledge he could take those actions
which appeared conducive for better serving the
king and assuring the security of this presidio.

I have requested the governor of Havana to
provide the galley and other ships as support for
the galiots which defend the entrance of this bar
in case the enemy comes to lay siege to this pre-

sidio. The Lieutenant General [governor of Cuba] sent this galley with a 106-man crew. It entered the harbor on the 4th of this month. Happily there were no enemy vessels nearby to see it until it had dropped anchor in the bay. For now that is what I wish to bring to Your Excellency's attention so that Your Excellency can inform the King.

I desire that God guard the esteemed person of Your Excellency for many years.

St. Augustine, Florida, April 13, 1743

Your most obedient servant,
Don Manuel Montiano
[rubric]

Montiano's superiors were outraged at his cowardice and indecisive action. After consultation with Philip V, Campillo bitterly rebuked the Florida governor. He accused Montiano of not doing his best to maintain the security of the presidio and of neglecting his responsibilities by not taking reprisals on the English and their Indian allies when they appeared near the fort. In Campillo's view, Oglethorpe had taught Montiano and his men a good lesson, and the next time the king hoped the Florida garrison would be better prepared to face an attack.[58] Montiano was in no better standing with the governor of Cuba, Juan Francisco de Güemes y Horcasitas. Güemes had sent reinforcements—300 men under Lieutenant Colonel Juan Pichón—and other kinds of aid, but to no good purpose. He saw little hope that the incompetent Montiano could accomplish anything against Oglethorpe, who had already shown up Montiano's ineptitude at Bloody Marsh. As a result Güemes was recalling Pichón and his men. In one last word he stated angrily: "Your

Excellency should understand how disagreeable
these events are for me because of the way in
which steps were taken to overturn what I intended and conceived and put forward for the
best interests of the king."[59] In short, Montiano
had not fulfilled his responsibilities. But he was
not recalled. In fact he stayed on in Florida six
more years, strengthening the defenses of the presidio and improving relationships with the Indians. When he left St. Augustine in 1749, he was
actually rewarded with the governorship of Panama and the presidency of the audiencia[60] there,
evidence that his superiors had short memories.[61]

Although only an episode in the larger contest
for empire in the Southeast, the Oglethorpe raid
in March, 1743 marked the end of an era. First,
after 1743 no more serious attempts were made
either from Georgia or from Carolina to dislodge
the Spaniards from their positions in St. Augustine, Apalache, and Pensacola. In fact one English officer stated forlornly, the Spaniards "make
the greatest Jest, Burlesque, and ridicule of all
our Expeditions from Cartagena to Augustine."
Second, the lessening of tension between Florida
and the English colonies after 1743 reflected a
shift in the balance of power in the Southeast.
The English had learned—by hard experience—
that they could not uproot the Spaniards in Florida, yet they could contain them within the confines of the Florida peninsula. Now a more serious
threat came from the French in Mobile and
Natchez and from their *coureurs des bois* working
among the Indians in the interior. Third, the Indians themselves began changing their stance in
the face of the three-cornered imperial struggle
in the Southeast. From Queen Anne's War to the

Oglethorpe raid in 1743, the English had dominated the Indians, won them over as allies, and used them effectively against the Spaniards. Occasionally there were defections, like the Yamasee in 1715, but overall the Carolinians and Georgians were masterful in gaining the friendship of the natives. After 1743, however, the Indians began to see the advantages of playing off the English against the Spaniards or French, to accept offers for their friendship or neutrality from the highest bidder. And the Indians often changed their minds. This helped the governor in St. Augustine, and the number of Indian raids declined sharply. In the end Montiano and his successors were able to strengthen their hold on Spanish Florida. In fact, by 1763 when a diplomats' treaty turned the colony over to the English, Florida was in a stronger defensive position than ever before.[62] The Spaniards had prevailed in the face of many adversities.

JOHN JAY TePASKE

Duke University

Notes.

1. The standard general account of the discovery and colonization of Florida to 1574 is still Woodbury Lowery, *The Spanish Settlements within the Present Limits of the United States, 1513–1574*, 2 vols. (New York, 1901, 1905). On the French in Florida one should consult Charles E. Bennett, *Laudonnière and Fort Caroline: Documents and History* (Gainesville, Fla., 1964). David L. Dowd reviews the historiography of the French in Florida in the introduction to Jean Ribaut, *The Whole & True Discovery of Terra Florida* (Gainesville, Fla., 1964), a facsimile edition of the London publication of 1563. Another useful reprint (of the 1587 edition) is René Laudonnière, *A Notable History Containing Four Voyages Made by Certain French Captains into Florida*, ed. M. Basanier, trans. R. Hakluyt (Larchmont, N.Y., 1964).

See also René Laudonnière, *Three Voyages*, trans. Charles E. Bennett (Gainesville, Fla., 1975). For Pedro Menéndez de Avilés and the founding of Florida see Gonzalo Solís de Merás, *Pedro Menéndez de Avilés: Adelantado, Governor, and Captain-General of Florida*, trans. Jeannette Thurber Connor (DeLand, Fla., 1923); in the introduction to a facsimile edition of *Menéndez* (Gainesville, Fla., 1964) Lyle N. McAlister reviews the historiography of the Spanish in Florida; Michael V. Gannon, *The Cross in the Sand* (Gainesville, Fla., 1965); Bartolomé Barrientos, *Pedro Menéndez de Avilés, Founder of Florida*, trans. Anthony Kerrigan (Gainesville, Fla., 1965).

2. The best study on mission expansion is John Tate Lanning, *The Spanish Missions of Georgia* (Chapel Hill, N.C., 1935). See also the dissertation of Robert Allen Matter, "The Spanish Missions of Florida: The Friars versus the Governor in the Golden Age," University of Washington, Seattle, 1972; Matter, "Economic Basis of the Seventeenth-Century Florida Missions," and "Missions in the Defense of Florida," *Florida Historical Quarterly* 52 (July, 1973): 18–38, 54 (July, 1975): 18–38.

3. The source for this period is Verner W. Crane, *The Southern Frontier, 1670–1732* (Ann Arbor, Mich., 1929).

4. On the siege of 1740 see *Collections of the Georgia Historical Society*, vol. 7, pt. 1 (Savannah, 1909); *The Saint Augustine Expedition of 1740: A Report to the South Carolina General Assembly, Reprinted from the Colonial Records of South Carolina with an Introduction by John Tate Lanning* (Columbia, S.C., 1954); Larry E. Ivers, *British Drums on the Southern Frontier: The Military Colonization of Georgia, 1733–1749* (Chapel Hill, N.C., 1974), pp. 90–132; John Jay TePaske, *The Governorship of Spanish Florida* (Durham, N.C., 1964), pp. 139–46.

5. For the Spanish invasion of Georgia see Ivers, *British Drums*, pp. 151–73; TePaske, *Governorship of Spanish Florida*, pp. 146–52; *Collections of the Georgia Historical Society*, vol. 7, pt. 3 (Savannah, 1913).

6. *Dictionary of National Biography* (*DNB*), s.v., "Kimber, Edward."

7. Sidney A. Kimber, "The 'Relation of a Late Expedition to St. Augustine,' with Biographical and Bibliographical Notes on Isaac and Edward Kimber," in *The Papers of the Bibliographical Society of America* (Chicago, 1934), 28:81–96; Kimber's introduction to *A Relation, or Journal, of a Late Expedition to the Gates of St. Augustine, on Florida* (Boston, 1935), pp. iii–viii, a reprint of the 1744 edition. Leonard L. Mackall, "The Wymberley Jones De Renne Georgia Library by Its Librarian," *Georgia Historical Society* 2 (June, 1918): 63–86. Frank Gees Black, "Edward Kimber: Anonymous Nov-

elist of the Mid-Eighteenth Century," *Harvard Studies and Notes in Philology and Literature* 17 (1935): 27–42.

8. Alexander Chalmers, ed., *The General Biographical Dictionary: Containing an Historical and Critical Account of the Lives and Writings of the Most Eminent Persons in Every Nation; particularly the British and Irish; from the Earliest Accounts to the Present Time* (London, 1815), 19:348–49.

9. S. Kimber, "Biographical Notes," p. 94.

10. Chalmers, *Biographical Dictionary*, p. 349; *DNB*, s.v. "Kimber, Isaac."

11. Chalmers, *Biographical Dictionary*, p. 349.

12. Ibid., pp. 348–49; *DNB*; S. Kimber, "Biographical Notes," pp. 94–96.

13. *DNB*.

14. S. Kimber, "Biographical Notes," p. 82; Black, "Anonymous Novelist," p. 80.

15. S. Kimber, "Biographical Notes," pp. 82–83. This article contains a copy of Edward Kimber's notations on his itinerary in America.

16. Edward Kimber, "Itinerant Observations in America, Reprinted from the London Magazine, 1745–46," in *Collections of the Georgia Historical Society* (Savannah, 1878), 4:15–18.

17. S. Kimber, "Biographical Notes," p. 83.

18. When originally published, the "Observations" were out of order and did not follow Edward Kimber's original itinerary in America. Kimber points this out in a note in the "Observations," pp. 63–64.

19. E. Kimber, "Observations," p. 10; succeeding references (page numbers) to this source appear within parentheses in the text.

20. S. Kimber, "Biographical Notes," p. 83.

21. Ibid., p. 88.

22. Listed are the titles and dates of publication of Kimber's novels. *The Life and Adventures of Joe Thompson: A Narrative Founded on Fact; Written by Himself*, 2 vols. (London, 1750). *The History of the Life and Adventures of Mr. Anderson; Containing His Strange Variety of Fortune in Europe and America; Compiled from His Own Papers* (London, 1754). *The Life and Adventures of James Ramble, Esq.; Interspersed with the Various Fortunes of Certain Noble Personages Deeply Concerned in the Northern Commotions in the Year 1715; From His Own Manuscript*, 2 vols. (London, 1754). *The Juvenile Adventures of David Ranger, Esq.; From an Original Manuscript Found in the Collection of a Late Noble Lord*, 2 vols. (London, 1756). *The Life and Extraordinary Adventures of Capt. Neville Frowde of Cork; Written by Himself* (London, 1758). *The Happy Orphans: An Authentic History of Persons in High Life*, 2 vols. (London, 1759). *Maria: The Genuine Memoirs of an Admired*

[xliii]

Lady of Rank and Fortune and Some of Her Friends (London, 1764). *The Generous Briton, or the Authentic Memoirs of William Goldsmith, Esq.*, 2 vols. (London, 1765). See also Black, "Anonymous Novelist," for a full discussion of the novels—their literary merit and place in English life in the mid-eighteenth century.

23. Black, "Anonymous Novelist," pp. 28–29.

24. Ibid., pp. 36–42.

25. S. Kimber, "Biographical Notes," pp. 88–90.

26. *DNB*; S. Kimber, "Biographical Notes," pp. 88–94, which lists most of what Edward Kimber wrote and edited and in some cases gives the sums of money he received for his work.

27. E. Kimber, *Relation*, pp. 34–35.

28. James Oglethorpe to the Duke of Newcastle, Frederica, April, 1737, London, Public Record Office, Colonial Office Records, 5:654, pt. 1 (hereafter cited as CO).

29. Testimonio sobre haber arribado a este presidio tres Ingleses fugitivos de las colonias, vecinos de esta nación: año de 1738, August 23, 1738, Seville, Spain, Archivo General de Indias (hereafter AGI), Santo Domingo, Legajo 2541.

30. Carta del gobernador de la Florida al rey, March 10, 1740, ibid.

31. James Oglethorpe to the Duke of Newcastle, Frederica, November 15, 1739, CO 5:654, pt. 1.

32. James Oglethorpe to the Duke of Newcastle, Frederica, January 22, 1739/40, CO 5:654, pt. 1; see also Ivers, *British Drums*, pp. 92–104.

33. See Ivers, *British Drums*, pp. 105–32; TePaske, *Governorship of Spanish Florida*, pp. 139–46.

34. E. Kimber, *Relation*, p. 34.

35. TePaske, *Governorship of Spanish Florida*, pp. 146–52; Ivers, *British Drums*, pp. 151–61.

36. E. Merton Coulter, *A Short History of Georgia* (Chapel Hill, N.C., 1933), p. 48.

37. Quoted by Coulter, ibid.

38. Ivers, *British Drums*, pp. 174–75.

39. Ibid., p. 176.

40. E. Kimber, *Relation*, pp. 6–7; Ivers, *British Drums*, p. 176.

41. E. Kimber, *Relation*, p. 10.

42. Ivers, *British Drums*, p. 177; Carta del gobernador de la Florida a Don José del Campillo, St. Augustine, April 13, 1743, AGI, 87–3–12, no. 60, in the Stetson Collection, P. K. Yonge Library of Florida History, University of Florida, Gainesville (hereafter cited as Stetson Collection).

43. Ivers, *British Drums*, pp. 177–78.

44. Ibid., pp. 179–81; AGI, 87–3–12, no. 60, Stetson Collection.

45. Ivers, *British Drums*, p. 181.

46. Ibid.

47. AGI, 87–3–12, no. 60, Stetson Collection.

48. Ivers, *British Drums*, pp. 181–83.

49. Ibid.

50. Carta del gobernador de la Florida a Don José del Campillo, St. Augustine, December 7, 1742, AGI, 87–3–12, no. 55, Stetson Collection.

51. Testimonio del Cacique Pedro Chislala, St. Augustine, December 4, 1743, ibid.

52. Carta del gobernador de Cuba a Don José del Campillo, Havana, April 4, 1743, AGI, 87–3–12, no. 57, Stetson Collection.

53. Ibid.

54. Carta de los oficiales reales de la Florida al rey, St. Augustine, July 19, 1743, AGI, 58–1–34, no. 76, Stetson Collection; see also AGI, 87–3–12, no. 57, Stetson Collection.

55. Carta del gobernador de la Florida al rey, St. Augustine, March 20, 1743, AGI, 87–3–12, no. 51, Stetson Collection; see also Carta del Pedro Ruíz de Olano al rey, March 20, 1743, AGI, 87–3–12, no. 115, Stetson Collection.

56. AGI, 87–3–12, no. 60, Stetson Collection. The discrepancies in dates between Montiano's account and Kimber's narrative may be explained by the difference in calendars. The English used the Julian calendar, the Spanish, the Gregorian. Translation by J. J. T.

57. Here Domingo de la Cruz refers to an agreement between the Spanish and English that during any exchange of prisoners there be absolutely no contact between the sailors or officers effecting the exchange. This was intended as a means of preventing Protestant heresy from penetrating Florida.

58. Carta de Don José del Campillo a Don Manuel de Montiano, gobernador de la Florida, San Ildefonso, October 11, 1743, AGI, 87–3–12, no. 60, Stetson Collection.

59. Carta del gobernador de Cuba a Don José del Campillo, Havana, June 4, 1743, AGI, 87–3–12, no. 48, Stetson Collection.

60. An audiencia was a court of appeals and advisory body for the governor in Panama.

61. Despacho del rey al gobernador de la Florida, November 15, 1748, AGI, Santo Domingo, Legajo 2541.

62. For Spanish defense and Indian policy in Florida after 1743, see TePaske, *Governorship of Spanish Florida*, pp. 154–57, 214–26.

A

RELATION,

O R.

JOURNAL,

Of a late

EXPEDITION to the Gates
of St. *Augustine*, on *Florida:*

Conducted by

The Hon. General JAMES OGLETHORPE,
with a Detachment of his Regiment, &c.
from *Georgia.*

In a LETTER to the Reverend
Mr. ISAAC K------R in *London.*

By a Gentleman, Voluntier in the said Expedition.

L O N D O N:
Printed for T. ASTLEY, at the *Rose,* in St. *Paul's
Church-Yard.* M.DCC.XLIV.

A

RELATION,

O R

JOURNAL,

Of a late

EXPEDITION, &c.

Camp, at *Frederica, July* 29, 1743.

Dear and Honoured Sir,

TO make amends for the many Imperti-
nencies I have utter'd in the epiftolary
Way, fince I have been abfent from
Great Britain; I fhall honour my felf,
by relating to you a late Expedition
we have made on *Florida*, under our great and
good General; an Expedition, you will find, as
great in its Formation, as important in its Defign;
and as falutary in its Effects, to this Frontier Colony, and the whole *North America*, as it was bold
and hazardous in its Execution. And tho' the
rankling Malice of a few vagabond *Carolinians*
hath, in publick Papers, dar'd to infult their Pre-
ferver and Saviour, on the Account of that Incurfion; yet the difcerning Eyes my Lines will
be fubmitted to, will brufh off the Filth of Prejudice and Defamation, and either make them
afham'd of their Ignorance, or dread the Effects
of their impotent Efforts, to taint the Reputation
of the Man, who has fo lately fav'd them from

Fire

Fire and Sword, and ftood between them and all the Miferies of a powerful Invafion.

You will perceive, in the Courfe of my Letter, the various and uncommon Hardfhips, our Way of making War in *America* fubjects us to; Hardfhips equal to thofe, that the Soldiers of *Cato* endur'd amongft the parch'd Sands of *Libya*; or thofe of *Charles* XII. among the dreary, frozen Forefts of *Ruffia*; Hardfhips unknown, nor thought of, in your modifh Campaigns in *Flanders*; and capable, on the bare Reflexion, to fhock the Soul of a *H---p---k* Hero. What are our Tents; but the firft fpreading Beach, or rifing Sand-hill, or perhaps, now and then, the fuperior Comfort of a lofty Tree, or a Palmetto Shade; whilft the hardeft Marches, beneath the Fire of the Mid-day Sun, are fucceeded with unwholefome, noxious Dews, attended with Vermin of all Sorts, that poifon Reft? Our Drink, not even the tranflucent Wave; but the firft muddy Marfh-Water we can find, or perhaps Water little frefher than that from the Sea. Our Provifions, carried on our Backs; unattended with Baggage-Waggons, or Sumpter Horfes; our Officers without any Equipages, but their Swords and their Partifans; and a General himfelf, partaking the fame Fatigue as the meaneft Soldier: Yet under all this, a Chearfulnefs feldom difcover'd in Soldiers, and a Flow of Spirits, uninfpir'd by any Thing, but a natural Vivacity and Courage, and a temperate and hardy Way of living; an Ardour for Battle, that is inexpreffible, and difcovers it felf in the Eyes of the meaneft Centinel. This is a fhort Trait of General *Oglethorpe*'s undaunted Regiment; of whom it may be faid, with *Addifon*,

The War's whole Art, each private Soldier knows;
And with a General's Thirft of Conqueft glows.

[5]

General *Oglethorpe*, after the brave Defeat of the formidable Invasion of *Georgia*, by the *Spaniards*, in *July* 1742, receiv'd repeated Advices of their Preparations for another and more powerful Attempt on that Colony; for which they were provided with Transports, at the *Havannah*, and *Augustine*, and were beating up for Voluntiers all over *Mexico* and *Peru*. The Governor of the *Havannah* was to command in the Expedition, and his Excellency had private Information, that they would be at least ten thousand strong. He at the same Time had Information, that their late Losses had much weaken'd the Garison of *Augustine*, who were daily expecting Recruits and Provisions from *Old Spain*, the latter of which they were also in Distress for; notwithstanding which, they had form'd a Camp at *Diego*. To divert the sanguine Hopes of the *Spaniards* to make a Conquest of this Province; to shew them that he was still alive, and as undaunted at the Head of his Handful of Men, as they could be with their Thousands; to confine them and pen them up within the Walls of their Castle, by harrassing them with continual Alarms, and thereby inducing them to believe he had had powerful Assistances from Home; and to deter them from attempting again to visit a Spot, which had been so fatal to them, was his Excellency's laudable Design, in undertaking the Incursion of *March* 1743; when, with an unheard-of Boldness, he penetrated fifty Miles into the Enemy's Country, encamp'd under the very Walls of the Castle of *Augustine*, beat up their Out-Centries, and insulted a Garison of two or three thousand Men, without their daring to shew themselves out of their Cover; and all this perform'd with only two hundred regular Troops, and about three hundred Provincial Forces, by Sea and Land. So terrible is the Name of *Oglethorpe*, and so truly baneful

his

his Regiment to the *Spaniards* in *America!* 'Tis plain, from the Belief this Expedition gave them, that we were re-inforc'd, and in high Spirits and good Condition to receive them, they put off their intended Invafion for another Year; in which Time, we may have the Happinefs of his Excellency's returning with fuch Supports, as will not only defend us from their moft powerful Attempts, but retort upon them the Mifchiefs they have done to this Colony.

On *Saturday, Feb.* 26, 1742-3, The Detachment of the Regiment, intended for the Expedition on *Florida,* appear'd under Arms at *Frederica*; when their Arms and Accoutrements were examined, and every one receiv'd his Complement of Cartages, and was order'd to provide himfelf with a Haver-Sack and Water-Bottle, for the March. Afterwards they march'd out of the Town, and each Platoon fir'd at a Mark, before his Excellency, for the Prize of a Hat and Matchet, to the Man who made the beft Shot at an hundred Yards Diftance, in the Foffe round the Fortifications. He afterwards gave Beer to the Soldiers, and order'd the Whole to be ready to proceed by nine the next Morning.

A Command of Men, two Days before, was embark'd on board the Ship *Succefs,* Capt. *Thomfon,* who this Day went over the Bar, to cruize off *Auguftine.*

If in the Sea-faring Part of this Journal, Sir, you perceive a Difference of Stile, ufual to that Profeffion; you will find the Diverfity not unentertaining, when Things of that Kind can't well be deliver'd in another, or better Dialect.

Sunday, Feb. 27. The whole Detachment, Rangers, &c. embark'd on board the Guard Schooner *Walker,* Capt. *Davis,* and the two hir'd Schooners,

Sea-

Sea-Flower and *Elizabeth*, at ten in the Morning, under the following Officers; *viz.* Capt. *William Horton*; Lieut. *Paul Demere*, Lieut. *James Wall*; Enfign *Samuel Mac Kay*, Enfign *Sol. Chamberlaine*, Enfign *Peter Mercier*, Enfign *White Outerbridge*, Enfign *John Stewart*: And with them, Adjutant *William Robinfon*, Quarter-Mafter *Thomas Rofendale*, Mr. *Patrick Hourtein*, Commiffary. At two, Weigh'd, and fell down below the *Point-Guard*, faluting the Town with twenty-one Guns; Wind S. W.

Monday, Feb. 28. At feven, A. M. Weigh'd again, with little Wind at N. At eight, P. M. came to an Anchor, beyond *Jekyl-Creek* *.

Tuefday, March 1. At fix, A. M. Weigh'd again, and at Noon ftruck on a Bank near the *Dividers*; (where, as, in fhort, all over the Country, are many Banks of excellent Oyfters;) but foon got off; and the Wind blowing hard at W. N. W. we could not clear the Banks; but the Schooners in Company got to *Fort-William*, from whence Capt. *Horton* fent us a Pilot.

Wednefday, March 2. At one, A. M. We weigh'd with a frefh Gale at N. W. but, foon after, ftruck on a Mud-Bank, where we lay till eight, and then hove off, with the Tide of Flood, and got under Sail, with the Wind at N. N. E. (The Reafon of our

* *Jekyl-Ifland*, from whence this Creek derives its Name, is oppofite to the South End of St. *Simon*'s, and makes with it the Entrance from Sea into St. *Simon*'s Sound. The Creek is a Strait, between that and St. *Andrew*'s Sound; fo called, from a Settlement of that Name, formerly on the *Ifland of Cumberland*, which it wafh'd. It is the Property of Capt. *Horton*, whofe Houfe and Cattle thereon, were deftroy'd by the late Invafion. The Defcription of one of thefe Iflands infers that of all the reft, and in fhort, of the whole Colony: So that I fhall not en-large here, but defer any Thing on that Head, till I fend you an Account at large of *St. Simon's Ifland*. A few Rangers are at prefent fettled on *Jekyl*. It is about nine Miles long, and three Miles and an half broad.

our fo frequently running a-ground, was the extreme Length of our Veffel, which was too long to tack in thefe Inland-Straits, where the Channel is very narrow ; tho' the Sounds, as they are call'd, are almoft large enough to bear the Appellation of Seas.) At Noon, the General, Lieut. *Goldfmith*, and Enfign *Wanfele*, with a Detachment from the *Virginian* Recruits ; and Capt. *Carr*, with Part of his Marine Company *, appear'd in Sight, and pafs'd us ; and fome Time after, Lieut. *Maxwell*, his Excellency's Aid-de-Camp, Lieut. *Charles Mac Kay*, with Part of the Highland Provincial Company, and feventy-five of the *Indian* Warriors, in the fmall Perriaguas and Scout-Boats. At two, P. M. we came to an Anchor off *Fort-William* on *Cumberland-Ifland* †, and join'd the reft of the Fleet: Little Wind N. N. E. and fmall Rain.

Thurfday,

* This Provincial Company is quarter'd at their Captain's fine Plantation, call'd the *Hermitage*, on the Main, about twenty Miles from *Frederica*, which is defended, fince it was deftroy'd by the *Spaniards*, by four Quadrangular Wooden-Forts. His Lieutenant is Mr. *Kenneth Bailey*, who was taken Prifoner at *Moufa*, and efcap'd from *Old Spain* to *England*. At the fame Time was taken alfo, Capt. *John More Mackintofh*, of the Highland Company mentioned above, now in *England*, Enfign *Ronald Mac Donald*, and Mr. *James Mac Queen*.

† *Cumberland-Ifland* is about ten Miles S. W. of *St. Simon's*, and is, perhaps, the moft pleafingly fruitful Ifland on the Frontiers ; it is oppofite to *Amelia*, and the Main, and is wafh'd on one Side by the Ocean, and on the other, by St. *Andrew*'s and *Amelia* Sounds. Formerly a Part of it was fettled by the General, and was call'd St. *Andrew*'s, *&c.* being defended by a fmall wooden Fort, which was deftroy'd laft Summer by the *Spaniards*. Some Rangers are, at prefent, quarter'd on that Spot. The Shores, as all thofe of *America*, and particularly of this Part, prefent you with the View of a fine Beach, rifing into a Ridge of Sand-Hills, and terminating the Sight with thick Woods, or green Marfhes, which are not altogether unentertaining in Profpect. At the South Extremity of the Ifland is feated *Fort-William*; which, when the *Spaniards* came before it, was only a rude quadrangular Houfe, furrounded with Logs or Puncheons, and quite unprovided for a Defence againft a numerous Enemy:

How-

Thurfday, March 3. This Morning Orders came for the Forces to land for Refrefhment; and the Sea-Officers went to found the Bar, which oppofes it felf to the Entrance by Sea into this Harbour, call'd *Amelia* Sound. This twenty-four Hours, for the moft Part dark and hazy Weather, with fmall Rain and N. E. Winds; the reft fine and clear, with little Winds S. S. E.

Friday, March 4. The Officers and their Detachments land this Morning, with all their Arms and Accoutrements. At ten, Lieut. *Demeré*, and Enfign *Stewart*, with the Grenadiers, are boated over the Sound, and encamp on the Ifland *Amelia* *; where *Scrugs* and *Williams*, with the Rangers, were encamp'd before. Eleven P. M. The General and

B   his

However, the *Spaniards*, after attacking it for three Hours, with fixteen Sail of Ships and Galleys, and firing inceffantly, (which was anfwer'd from within, with what Cannon and Small-Arms they had,) thought proper to fheer off. Enfign *Alexander Stewart* commanded the fifty Men in the Fort, the reft being order'd to *Frederica*, under Enfign *Thomas Goldfmith*, now a Lieutenant, ere the *Spaniards* appear'd before the Fort. It is now repair'd and new Works added to it, fo as to make it a ftrong enough Place. It has two eighteen Pounders, on a Ravelin before the Fort, upon curious moving Platforms, that they can bring to bear any Way; a four Pounder, and fome Swivels. The Outworks of the Fort are, in Form, a regular Pentagon; the Rampart twelve Foot high, and about fifteen Foot thick, of Sand, fupported by Puncheons. The Charge is committed to Mr. *Stuart*, now a Lieutenant, who for his Bravery and Conduct was commiffion'd its Fort-Major. It is garifon'd by about fifty Men, and fix Non-commiffion'd Officers, under an Officer; who are every Month reliev'd from *Frederica*, the Head-Quarters of the Regiment. It entirely commands the moft Southerly Entrance into *Georgia*, and is about feventy Miles from St. *Auguftine*, and forty from *Frederica*. This Ifland is about twenty-five Miles long, and twelve broad.

* The Ifland *Amelia* is an uninhabited Ifland, about nineteen Miles long, and four broad, full of Game, and wild Beafts. St. *George*'s, and *Talbot*'s, which will alfo be mention'd, are two other fmall defert Iflands to the South, oppofite to St. *Wan*'s; on the former of which was a Fort, at the firft Settling of the Colony. Our Rangers frequently fcour thefe Iflands.

his Retinue, with the Officers, Recruits, Rangers, and *Indians*, fail'd in the fmall Craft, for *St. Juan's*, from whence they frequently fend out Parties for Intelligence.

Saturday, March 5. The Grenadiers being order-ed from *Amelia*, Capt. *Horton* review'd the De-tachment on the Parade behind the Fort. At three after Noon, an Exprefs arrived from the General, with Advice that all was well. At eight, another Exprefs arrived to the Commander in Chief.

Sunday, March 6. At ten in the Morning *S. Cole-man*, one of his Excellency's Servants, arriv'd Ex-prefs, and inform'd us, that the General and his whole Corps were arriv'd fafe at *St. Wan's*, where they were encamp'd; and that the *Indians* were gone to *Augustine*, in order to knap Prifoners, and gain Intelligence. At eleven, the Detachment em-bark'd again, being oblig'd to wade to the Boats up to their Middles, the Wind fetting on Shore. At twelve, a Ship was feen off the Bar, which fent in its Yawl, and prov'd to be the *Succefs*, Capt. *Thomfon*, who inform'd us, he had met with a feventy, and fixty Gun Ship, the *Kent*, and *York*, Captains *Coates* and *Mitchell*, who were order'd from *Jamaica*, to cruize for a Galleon and Pay-Ship, from the *Havannah*, bound to St. *Augustine*. Wind tort at S. W. In our old Birth all this Night.

Monday, March 7. Six P. M. we weigh with our Conforts; at ten, ftand over *Amelia* Bar, to Sea, with frefh Gales at W. and flying Clouds, and fteer E. S. E. Eight Feet the moft fhoal Water, on the Bar, at half Flood. At two, P. M. come to an Anchor clofe to *St. Juan's* Bar; at three, P. M. the General's Cutter came off to us, with *David Fellows*, his Cockfwain, and the Crew, to help us in: at five D°, the General came off, in his other Cutter, and order'd us to ftand in with

I   the

the Morning Flood. It continues blowing very hard all Night. We fee many Fires up the Country, which we take to be Signals of Alarm by the Enemy.

Tuefday, March 8. This Morning the Wind blowing very hard at N. W. we hous'd our Guns, and lafh'd our two nine Pounders to the Maft, putting our Swivels into the Hold. We got down our Fore-Top-Sail, Crofs-Jack, and Crotchet-Yards, and made every Thing ready, left we fhould be drove from our Anchors, and blown out to Sea. At Night more moderate, Wind W. and N. W.

Wednefday, March 9. This Morning the Wind being moderate at N. W. *Fellows* went afhore in the Cutter, and brought off Word, that the General had been alarm'd by five or fix Guns having been fir'd; but finding that we could not get in, fent Word he would affift us, when the Weather permitted, which we hope will foon. At nine A. M. his Excellency came off with two other Boats, to tow us in: He himfelf founded the Bar, feveral Times; but finding, that the Sea ran high, and there was but eight or nine Feet Water, we ftay'd till Time of half Flood. At ten, Wind at N. E. and hazy Weather; we lying clofe to the Bar, and two Sand-Hills bearing W. Southerly. At Noon we all weigh'd and got in, with little Winds at E. N. E. and hazy. We fteer'd in W. W. by N. and W. N. W. nine or ten Fathom Water, and came to Anchor about a Mile within the Bar. Fires and Smokes all up the Country. *Williams,* and fome of his Rangers are fent over to St. *George*'s. Plcafant Weather, with little Wind, at S. S. E.

It may not, here, feem impertinent, to remark a Circumftance, which may appear pretty odd in

Europe; which is, that the Soldiers of this Regiment are, perhaps, alfo, as good Sailors as there are to be met with; fome, in particular, really underftanding that Profeffion from its very Principles. This Knowledge is acquir'd by the many Marine and Boat-Services they have been engag'd in; for, his Excellency has not only conftantly harrafs'd the Enemy by Land, but has perpetually terrify'd them by his Sea-Cruizes, boldly attacking all their Veffels that came in his Way; in which Expeditions, his Soldiers have been detach'd, and have, frequently, either bang'd or plunder'd the *Spaniards*. A Sloop of their taking you have now in *England*, which brought to *Europe* Capt. *George Dunbar*, and Lieut. *Cadogan*, of this Regiment. The many Boat-Services are occafion'd by the Situation of this Southern Frontier, divided into a Parcel of Iflands, on which feparate Commands are ftation'd, or frequently fent; which require many little Voyages; the Particulars of fome of which, and the Accidents that have happen'd in them, would afford much Entertainment. Join'd to the Qualities of the good Soldier, and able Sailor, they are, alfo, expert Fifhers, and moft excellent Huntfmen; Characters of great Importance, and abfolutely neceffary in this Country. In one Week, at *Fort-William*, only four Men of the Command, purely for Diverfion, caught, to my Knowledge, with Lines, fifteen hundred Weight of Fifh; as, Bas, (which is as large as a Salmon) Mullet, Drum, and Slingre: And this is very common.

On *Wednefday, March* 9. At two in the Afternoon, we landed at St. *Mathia's* on *Florida*; and, after being review'd, (and the General's making a Speech, in which he gave us an Account of the Expedition we were upon;) his Excellency order'd fome Barrels of Beer to be given to the
Soldiers;

Soldiers; when we took up our Quarters on the other Side of a Sand-Hill, or Ridge, overgrown with Palmettos, and divers Kinds of Weeds, in a Savannah, defended on all Sides by a Wood; whose only Vacuities were some few Glades, made by the Entrance of a Creek, which in several Meanders gently roll'd its Waves from its Source, the River *St. Wan's*, till it enter'd the Lake *de Poupa*, now called *Oglethorpe's* Lake. At one End of this Savannah, the nearest to the Entrance of the Lake, and on the River Side of the Sand-Hills, the General fix'd his Head-Quarters; his Tent, by Day, being a Kind of an Alcove, that some neighbouring Shrubs had form'd on each Side; and his Retreat by Night, a Palmetto-Hut, which also held his Provisions, and other Lumber: His Servants building themselves Shades of Boughs, &c. on each Side of him. There did this great Man, seated on a Buffalo's Skin, pass the Hours, whilst encamp'd here, (which were vacant from his daily Journeys along the Beach, or in the neighbouring Woods, for Discoveries,) in instructive Lessons to the Officers and Gentlemen of his Detachment; and their Visit generally concluded with a Dinner, or Supper from his Kitchen, (a Wood-Fire in the Neighbourhood of his Hut,) compos'd of barbecu'd Pork, Poultry, which he had on board his Vessels; or Fish, of which large Quantities were catch'd in the aforesaid Creek, which ran before his Hut, and so pass'd, after several serpentine Turnings, into the Wood, on the contrary Side of the Savannah. At the other End of the Savannah, we clear'd a Passage, from *St. Juan's* Beach, into it, thro' a thick, mournful Wood, which had been robb'd of Leaves and Growth, by former *Indian* Fires; in which was placed an Advanc'd Guard of fifteen Men, and an Officer, whose Centries could discover,

ver, not only every Thing that approach'd us by Land, that Way, but, alfo, whatever pafs'd the Bar, or appear'd on the neighbouring Shores. On the Sand-Hills, South, and juſt by his Excellency's Quarters, our Main-Guard was poſted, whoſe Out-Centries could difcover all Veffels from the North-ward; and from whence, every Thing behind us might be defcry'd on its firſt Appearance. The Rangers were, with their Horfes, encamp'd in a fmall Clofe near the Soldiers of the Regiment; whilſt the new Recruits and Marines, with the Highlanders, either encamp'd on the Beach, or kept on board their refpective Boats. Whilſt in this Situation, our Men built themfelves fmall Huts, divided themfelves into feparate Meffes, and with the utmoſt Decorum enter'd into all the Œconomy of Families. The Woods fell at their repeated Strokes, for Firing and Building; and the whole Place began to look like an in-habited Country. Every Officer had a Hut, at the Head of his Platoon; and, fo, was ready to quell any Diforder that might arife. Their Pro-vifions confiſted of Rice, Beef, Flour, and Mo-loffes, which were deliver'd for two or three Days at a Time, by the Commiffary and Quarter-Mafter, from on board the Store-Schooner; where a Man of every Mefs repair'd to fetch it, for him-felf and Comrades. Their Drink was Water, as was the General's, and the reſt of the Officers, from the Wells we had dug round the Camp; which, to fay the beft of it, was brackifh, green, muddy and ftinking. Frequently, when bad Huf-bandry had exhauſted our Provifions before the Time of a Supply, our Men would go out to fifh, and oyfter: And lo! the whole Camp was over-fpread with the marine Inhabitants.

Thurfday, March 10. This Day Capt. *Thomfon* appear'd off *St. Juan's* Bar. All well in the Camp.

Fires

Fires up the Country, as ufual. 'Tis impoffible to exprefs, what a diftant gloomy Profpect, fo many Fires at a great Remotenefs in an Enemy's Country occafion: A Painter can only exprefs the Scene.

Friday, March 11. The Drums beat to Arms at nine, and we remain'd in that Pofture till twelve at Noon, expecting immediately to march; but had, then, Orders to retire to our Huts. The General's Policy was, and is, very obfervable, in the frequent Alarms his People receive, and the frequent Motions he obliges them to make; knowing very well, that the Ruft of Inactivity and Idlenefs too foon corrupts the Minds, and enervates the Body of the Soldier. To this are, perhaps, owing, the many different Fatigues, his Regiment goes thro' in *Georgia,* which he is always promoting; as, clearing Roads, draining Swamps, Marfhes, &c. which fo harden'd and ftrengthen'd the *Roman* Legions, who have left, from the Time of *Cæfar* to the Declenfion of their Empire, eternal Monuments of Induftry and Labour, in all the Countries they fubdu'd. At two o' Clock, a hard Rain (accompanied with repeated Lightnings, and Thunder-Claps, that are common in thefe Southern Climates, and are wonderfully fevere; the whole Element feeming to be kindled into a livid Flame, and all Nature meeting with a general Diffolution) fet in, and continued till we were thoroughly foak'd, and our Arms had received confiderable Damage. At four o' Clock, the *Cowhati Indians,* who went to *Auguftine,* after fo long Expectations, and divers Conjectures about their long Stay, return'd; bringing with them five Scalps, one Hand, which was cut off with the Glove on, feveral Arms, Clothes, and two or three Spades; which they had the Boldnefs to bring away, after having attack'd a Boat with upwards of forty
Men

Men in it, under the very Walls of the Caftle, killing about twenty of them, and over-fetting the reft; who alfo had met with Death, but for the continu'd Fire of their great Guns. It feems, that they were Pioneers, and were going, under an Officer, to dig Clay for the King's Works. We heard them long before they came in Sight, by the melancholy Notes of their warlike Death-houp. For the *Spaniards* having kill'd one of their People, they, as ufual with them in that Cafe, gave no Quarter, and therefore brought his Excellency no Prifoner; which was what he earneftly defir'd. To give you a lively Idea of what occurs here, of thefe Sons of the Earth, I premife fome Defcription of their Figure, Manners, and Method of making War. As to their Figure, 'tis generally of the largeft Size, well proportion'd, and robuft, as you can imagine Perfons nurs'd up in manly Exercifes can be. Their Colour is a fwarthy, copper Hue, their Hair generally black, and fhaven, or pluck'd off by the Roots, all round their Foreheads and Temples. They paint their Faces and Bodies, with Black, Red, or other Colours, in a truly diabolic Manner; or, to fpeak more rationally, much like the former uncultivated Inhabitants of *Britain*, whom *Tacitus* mentions. Their Drefs is a Skin or Blanket, tied, or loofely caft, over their Shoulders; a Shirt which they never wafh, and which is confequently greafy and black to the laft Degree; a Flap, before and behind, to cover their Privities, of red or blue Bays, hanging by a Girdle of the fame; Boots about their Legs, of Bays alfo; and what they call Morgiffons, or Pumps of Deer or Buffalo Skin, upon their Feet. Their Arms, and Ammunition, a common Trading-Gun; a Pouch with Shot and Powder; a *Tomohawk*, or Diminutive of a Hatchet, by their Side; a Scalping-Knife, Piftol, *&c.* But, however, you'll fee their
Drefs,

Drefs, by thofe the General has carry'd to *England*. As to their Manners, tho' they are fraught with the greateft Cunning in Life, you obferve little in their common Behaviour, above the brute Creation. In their Expeditions they hunt for their Provifion, and, when boiled or barbecu'd, tear it to Pieces promifcuoufly with their Fifts, and devour it with a remarkable Greedinefs. Their Drink is *Weé-tuxeé*, or Water, on.thefe Occafions; but, at other Times, any Thing weaker than Wine or Brandy, is naufeous to them; and they'll exprefs their great Abhorrence by fpitting it out, and feeming to fpew at it: All which is owing to the Lofs of their native Virtues, fince the *Europeans* have enter'd into all Meafures for trading with them; for, view them without Prejudice, you will perceive fome Remains of an ancient Roughnefs and Simplicity, common to all the firft Inhabitants of the Earth; even to our own dear Anceftors, who, I believe, were much upon a Level with thefe *Indian* hunting Warriors, whom his Excellency has fo tam'd, fince his being in *America*, and màde fo fubfervient to the Benefit of the *Englifh* Nation.

When they make an Incurfion into an Enemy`s Country, they decline the open Roads and Paths, and only fcout along the Defiles and Woods, ready to pop on any Prey that fhall appear in the open Country; whom they attack with terrible and mournful Cries, that aftonifh even more than their Arms. If none of their own Party is kill'd, they take Prifoners all they can lay Hands on; but if on the contrary, they give no Quarter. Before they go to War, they undergo the Ceremony of Phyficking, which is done very privately in the Recefles of fome hoary Wood, remote from the Eyes of any white Perfon; and generally employs a Day or two: Then performing the Ceremony

C   mony

mony of their War-Dance, they are ready to begin their Work. Thefe two laft mention'd Ceremonies feem to be a Mixture of the religious and the political. Their Medicine is a Kind of red Pafte, &c. &c. but of what made, the Lord above knows.

So much will ferve for the Purpofe of this Relation; and for a full Account of the religious and civil Affairs, &c. of thefe natural Sons of *America*, a farther Account of their Manners, and other entertaining and curious Articles, I refer you to the many good Accounts that have formerly been given, by many creditable Authors; or to a Converfation with a very worthy and agreeable young Gentleman, now in *England* with his Excellency, whom, I hope, you'll fee, *Thomas Marriotte*, Efq; who underftands thefe People better, than any one I ever knew.

Imagine to your felf a Body of fixty or feventy of thefe Creatures, marching in Rank and File, (and by their martial Figure, and Size, forming, or extending a Front equal to that of two hundred Men,) with the mournful Howls and Cries, ufual on the Occafion, and every now and then popping their Pieces off, which was anfwer'd by the Main-Guard, as they pafs'd, in a continually refum'd Fire. His Excellency was feated, to receive them, under fome neighbouring Trees, on a Buffalo's Skin, furrounded by his Officers; when every one approaching him, he fhook them by the Hand, welcom'd them home, in the *Indian* Tongue, and thank'd them for the Service they had done him. The War Captains, or old Men, he retain'd; who being feated, had three Hogs, Fifh, Oyfters, Bread, Beer, and divers other Refrefhments given them; when they inform'd his Excellency, there was no Camp at *Diego*: And then his Excellency propos'd their marching again to *Auguftine*, with him and his People;

ple;

ple; but, whether they had been handled more feverely than they reprefented, or, whether they were terrify'd with the great Guns, &c. they feem'd not much inclin'd to it; and feeing that the General ufed a few Perfuafions for that End, they objected to his fmall Number, told him, they could fhift well enough, but were not pleas'd with the white Mens Method of going to War. They knew, as they exprefs'd it in their Tongue, that his Men were angry and full of Blood; but their red Paffion would drive them into many Dangers, &c. They retir'd and made themfelves drunk, that Evening, and thought no more of their Loffes or Exploits. The General fitting among them, and acquiefcing with their Manners, in their Cups, they promis'd to march with him; but what they faid, feem'd forc'd, and he declin'd their Aid. The Nights are very cold, and the Dew wets us thro' and thro'; fo that we are oblig'd to keep Fires all round our Huts. The Difference between the intenfely heated Day, and the raw, chilly Night, attended with fuch heavy Dews, muft have a very noxious Influence upon the human Body.

Saturday, March 12. This Morning, Mr. *William Abbot* arrived Exprefs from Capt. Lieutenant *James Mac Kay,* Commanding-Officer at *Frederica,* in a Canoo, bringing a Packet, which arriv'd from *England,* by the Way of *Charles-Town,* for his Excellency. He acquaints us, all is well at home. We remain quietly in our Camp. The *Indians* want to return to *Frederica,* miffing their favourite Liquors; we having nothing to give them but Beer.

Sunday, March 13. *Abbot* is difpatch'd again to *Frederica.* Amongft his other News, he brought Word of the taking of one *Preber,* a *German,* in the *Creek* Nation, who had endea-

vour'd

vour'd to fet the *Indians* againſt the *Engliſh*, and
feemed, by fome Papers found on him, to be a
fubtil Jefuit Miffionary. He was brought five
hundred Miles, by Order of Capt. *Kent*, of *Fort
Auguſta*, to the General at *Frederica*, where he is
confined by Capt. *Mac Kay*. He will, no Doubt,
be heard much of in *England*; for he was natura-
lized in *Carolina*.

Monday, March 14. One *Combes* arrives from
Frederica in a Perriagua, who is immediately
clapp'd in Irons, by his Excellency's Order, on
board the *Walker*; he having trifled away his Time,
and, by making twelve *Indians*, who were coming
with him, drunk, occafion'd their ſtaying at *Amelia*,
from whence they returned to *Frederica*. At three
in the Afternoon, the *General* was beat thro' the
Camp; half an Hour after, the *Aſſembly*, and
immediately the *Troop*; when the whole prepared
to march. His Excellency left the Veffels at
Anchor off *St. Wan*'s; and, on board the *Walker*,
a Party commanded by Lieutenant *Thomas Gold-
ſmith*, to affiſt in fecuring his Retreat, if needful;
and the Sick, under the Charge of Mr. *Watkins*,
a Surgeon, Voluntier in the Expedition. Of all
the *Indians*, only four, *viz.* the famous *Tooanowi*,
Sloffkaw, and two more accompany'd us; the reſt
fetting off, in the Morning, for *Frederica*. At
four, we reach'd the Horfe-Guards, about a Mile
below our Camp, a Place on the Beach, where
the *Spaniards*, before the Siege of *St. Auguſtine*,
kept a Party of Cavalry, at a Look-out, which is
now deſtroy'd. At this Place, a Boat had landed
fome Barrels of Beer, which was diſtributed at a
Pint a Man; and fuch an unexpected Bounty
from the General, wonderfully elated the Soldiers.
We march'd briſkly from this Place, ſtill along
St. Juan's Beach, till the Cover of Night brought
us to the firſt Freſh-Water *Camena* (or Creek,

as

as 'tis call'd by our *Augustine* Veterans) where we
halted; and mounting the Sand-Hills, lay under
Arms, in a Bottom, between two Ridges, mounting a Double-Guard, till the next Morning. The
fiery Heat of the Sun, darting its Beams on us,
which were reflected back by the Sand, and almoft fcorch'd and blinded us, during this Afternoon's March of fourteen Miles, was fcarce bear-
able, by fuch of us, as were new ones at this
Trade; nor could we have ftood it, but that
the refrefhing Breeze from the Sea chear'd our
Spirits. The Water we brought in our Cantines,
and Bottles, was boiling hot; and our Arms burnt
us, when we touch'd the Steel. His Excellency,
and his Horfemen rode before; and in our Van,
march'd the Highlanders, and Capt. *Horton* with
his Grenadiers; whilft the Rear was brought up
by the new rais'd *Virginians*, under Enfign *Wanfel*.
In the Night the Sand blew on us from the Hills,
and, together with the hateful Dew, made our
Lodging more uncomfortable than can be de-
fcribed.

Tuefday, March 15. Arriving, after an Hour's
March, to the Road that leads to *Diego*, we ftruck
into it, from the Beach, and had then a Profpect
of the neighbouring Country. 'Twas with the ut-
moft Satisfaction, I furvey'd this Part of the fineft
Land in *North America*, which feem'd quite open,
and was only, here and there, diverfify'd with rifing
Hummocks of Trees and leafy Thickets, which
ferv'd to enliven the variegated Scene. In fhort, I
began to fancy myfelf in *Britain*, whofe Paftures and
Meadows are ftill fo frefh in my Mind; whilft an
Infinity of uncommon Birds were chanting their
wild Notes on every Bufh and Brake. Happy,
unhappy *Spaniards!* Poffefs'd of the fineft Countries in the World, you lofe them by your Covet-
oufnefs and Pride! Our Thirft, each Man's Wa-

ter

ter being expended, began to be very fevere; fo
that the General foon order'd an Halt in a Marfh,
where we refrefh'd with Provifion, and fuch muddy
Water as the Place afforded, at about ten o' Clock
in the Morning. Here it muft be noted, that
every Perfon carried his own Provifion, (in his
Knap-fack, or Haver-fack, on his Back, Officers
and Gentlemen not excepted,) of which, we had
for feven Days, at the Allowance of a Pound of
Bifcuit, and ten ounces of Cheefe *per* Man; which,
with Beef, if the Men chofe it, was, and is the
ufual Allowance. At one, we refum'd our Rout
(and by the Narrownefs of the Path were oblig'd to
march one a-breaft) thro' this fine fallow Country,
which, before the Siege of *Auguftine*, was replete
with lowing Kine, and bleating Flocks of Sheep;
but fince that, they allow no Settlements in the
Country, and keep all their Cattle on the
Matanças, continually in fear of another Invafion; leaving this fine Land defert and uncultivated. At three, we arriv'd at the Place, where
formerly the Houfe of Don *Diego Spinoza* ftood,
which was garifon'd by the *Spaniards*, and is com-
monly known by the Name of *Fort Diego*. It was
taken by the General, when he laid Siege to the
Caftle, and the Garifon and Owner of the Houfe
made Prifoners of War. There are ftill fome
Ruins of it left, as a great Crofs, Trench, and
Slaughter-Houfe for Cattle. It muft formerly
have been a very fine Eftate; but is now quite
deferted. In our Way to this Place, we march'd
thro' feveral Bogs and Swamps up to our Bellies.
At half an Hour after three, we reach'd a thick
Wood, (after having pafs'd a large Creek, at low
Water; which, had the Tide been in, would have
taken us up to the Neck,) where his Excellency
halted us, for fome Refrefhment, and where we
had Plenty of Water, thick, and ftinking enough,
from

from a neighbouring Marſh. His Excellency's
Prudence and Conduct is highly to be admir'd in
halting his Men at proper Times, in ſhady Places,
where Water may be had; which, indeed, is the
Secret of preſerving Men in theſe hot Climates;
and the contrary of which, perhaps, deſtroy'd ſo
many in the *Weſt-Indies*. Here our Men found
out the Contrivance of putting Orange-Peel into
their Bottles, which temper'd the Water's Heat,
and, by its generous Bitter, imparted a noble
Warmth to the Stomach. The Oranges were found
by the *Indians*, for they grow wild in this Country. The Heat of the Day being over, we march'd
thro' ſeveral ſcrubby Marſhes, and Savannahs, and
over a large Creek, which haply was at low Water,
till we arriv'd at a Kind of a Pine-barren (falſely
and abſurdly ſo call'd, from producing nothing
but thoſe Trees;) where we encamp'd, or rather
lay on our Arms, all Night; his Excellency taking
up his Quarters in a hollow Thicket, to the Right
of his People. All this Day's March, we ſaw the
melancholy Spots the *Indians* had ſet Fire to,
which, in ſome Places, had ſpread near a Mile,
deſtroying all before it, and leaving whole Foreſts
in Ruin. Theſe, it ſeems, were the Fires we diſcover'd at Sea; which were not made by the Enemy, but our own *Indians* : And following this
Policy, his Excellency ſet Fire to the Woods,
before we march'd from the aforeſaid Halting-
Place; that the Enemy might be deceived, and
think we were ſtill there. When we were ſettled
in our Encampment, a Number of Men were detach'd to dig Wells, for we ſtood in great Want
of Water; and ſeven or eight were immediately
ſunk, which ſupply'd us very well; but the Water
was brackiſh. We are in great Hopes the *Spaniards*
will come down upon us. Guard as uſual. Several
of the new Men, not being capable to hold out, were
ſent

fent back, under the Care of a Corporal. We
reckon our felves thirty Miles from *St. Wan*'s, and
twenty from *Anguftine*.

Wednefday, March 16. We continue our March,
till we arrive, at twelve at Noon, fcorch'd to
Death, and in great Want of Water, to a Place
call'd *the Grove*, which truly merits that Name;
where there is a running Brook of the fineft
Water I ever drank. In this Morning's March,
moftly thro' Pine-barrens, diverfify'd with many
entertaining Profpects, and the Sight of a Milli-
on of Paroquets and other Birds peculiar to the
Place, feveral of our Men fail'd, and were taken
up by the Horfes: It was fo hot, we were almoft
barbecu'd, and we met with no Water. Being fo
near the Enemy, his Excellency, in every open or
expos'd Place we march'd thro', order'd Captain
Horton to form us, and fo march in Rank and
File, as long as the broad Road continued.

This Brook, we are now folacing our felves by,
this charming reviving Rill, is feated between two
large Pine-barrens, in a Kind of a Bottom, which
is quite obfcure, from the Thickets that defend
it, on the Side of *Auguftine*; and on the other
Side, a moft delicious Grove of Cyprefs, Laurel,
&c. extends its leafy Honours, into the Air, af-
fording a fine, fhady Retreat, from the broiling
Beams of the Sun. Here our People, throwing
afide their Arms and Clothes, gave Way to the
pleafing Reft it afforded them; whilft the cryftal
Stream was inceffantly quaff'd, and every divert-
ing Difcourfe or mirthful Interlude, fo common
with Soldiers, took Place; which charm'd the General, who was delighted to fee the ufual, natural
Flow of Spirits in his Men, unaffifted by ought,
but a Vivacity and Chearfulnefs, infpir'd by native Courage, Vigour, and Health. 'Twas here,
that, feated under an Oak, his Excellency treated

I   his

his Officers, and other Gentlemen, with Ham, and a Glaſs of Wine each; but more particularly, with his pleaſing and inſtructive Diſcourſe. Two Inſtances of the Worth of his Regiment occurr'd at this Place, which I muſt not omit. One of the Soldiers ſcooping a Hornful of Water from the Brook, when we firſt arriv'd, cry'd out in a Rapture, Here's Sack! Sack, my Lads! The General pleaſed with the Fellow's Obſervation, call'd him to him, gave him a Piece of Money; and, mingling ſome Wine with his Water, drank to him. The other Inſtance ſhews the excellent Decorum they are under, and Readineſs to encounter all Dangers; and was this, that one of the Centries from the Guard, on the other Side of the Brook, had the Misfortune to have his Piece go off, at Half-Cock; inſtantly the Whole ſtarted up, and, without Diſorder or Confuſion, immediately form'd *themſelves*, under their ſeveral Officers, without the leaſt Word of Command.

At five, we again ſet forward, and march'd over a large, and prodigious long Pine-barren, (melted continually with the igneous Rays darting without Intermiſſion on our Heads,) which was ſo regular an one, as to appear more like a wide, extended, regular Grove, than ſo wild a Place. Half Way thro', ſuch a Stink aroſe, as almoſt ſtruck us all to the Ground, which no one could imagine the Source of; at laſt, a Pole-Cat, like ours in *Europe*, but more remarkable in its horrid Scent, was perceived, and kill'd, after a long Chace, by our Horſemen: This Circumſtance occaſion'd a great deal of Mirth. We had ſeveral Alarms in this Place; as, thinking we heard Guns fir'd, and Hallowing at a Diſtance; but diſcover'd nothing. We form'd on this Occaſion, four or five Times. Marching thro' the Woods is rather more incommodious than the Beach, on account of ſo many Stumps and Pal-

metto

metto Roots, as we meet with, which bruife our
Feet, and often occafion us to tumble down.   Towards Evening we came up to feveral Defiles of
Thickets, *&c.* which made us cautious of an Am-
bufcade ; but we pafs'd them, without being attack'd, and arriv'd in the broad High-Road
leading to *Auguftine*, at about eight o' Clock, ac-
counting ourfelves about one Mile from the Ruins
of the fatal *Moufa*, and three from *St. Auguftine.*
We ftruck off from the Road, into a Savannah
on the Right; where a Double-Guard being mounted, and Centries plac'd, we laid down on our
Arms, to take fome little Repofe, after fo long a
Day's March ; in the latter Part of which, we met
with no Water ; and here, when we dug Wells,
none could be had that was drinkable ; but, however, Neceffity obliging, we ftrain'd it from the
Mud, thro' our Teeth and Handkerchiefs; and,
in fome Meafure, thereby cool'd our heated
Throats.   Here we could plainly hear the Tattoo
beat in the Caftle of *St. Auguftine*, and our moft
advanc'd Centries could hear theirs challeng'd.
At three in the Morning, a falfe Alarm being
fpread, that one of the Guard had deferted, the
Adjutant was ordered filently to wake us, and
we march'd, with as great Circumfpection and
Caution as poffible, back to the Entrance of the
afore-mentioned Defiles, before the Break of Day,
the Grenadiers bringing up our Rear.

Thurfday, March 17. Halting at Day-Break, we
form'd, in a fmall Marfh, on both Sides enclos'd with
thick Woods; at whofe Entrance grew a Multitude
of large Palmettos.   Amongft them the General
ordered a Vacancy to be cut, in Form of an half
Moon, capable to conceal his Men from View;
and here he was refolv'd to wait for the Enemy,
if they fhould have the Courage to venture from
their Walls. Lieut. *James Wall* commanded an
Advanc'd-Guard, and was order'd to let the
Whole

Whole of their Number pafs, before he difcover'd himfelf, and then to attack them in the Rear, and drive them up into our Teeth; when, if they had ventur'd to come, five hundred could not have efcap'd Death. In this Station, we were al- moft devour'd with Vermin, and diftracted for Want of Water; which, after digging in the 'Wood, we could not find. His Excellency, and fix or feven Horfemen, in order to decoy them out, rode from hence as far as the Out-Centries of the *Spaniards*, who retir'd, without firing, into the Caftle, purfu'd by him to the very Walls. But find- ing nothing could provoke them to appear, he re- turned, propofing to lie in the fame Pofture for two or three Days, and to fend out frequent Parties to the very Gates of the Town. However, this De- fign was baulk'd, by the Defertion of one *Eels*, of Col. *Cook*'s Company; a Fellow, who was dif- contented, and knew our Number, Difpofition, and every Thing, which the Relation of could in- duce them to fally upon us. He was purfued, but had hid himfelf in the Woods; from whence, he afterwards went to the Enemy. Finding our Situation, by this, would be too dangerous, his Excellency order'd the Whole to march, himfelf always bringing up the Rear.

At eight o' Clock, we enter'd the long Pine-barren, when our *Indians* difcovered a fine, cool Spring, at the Root of a large Oak; the very Mention of which occafion'd feveral of our Men to defert their Arms, and run towards it; for which, two of them were tied Neck and Heels, as an Example to the reft. We all march'd up to this charming Place, this *Mofaic* Stream, gladen'd, as the *Ifraelites* were on a like Occafion; and after drinking and filling our Bottles, refum'd our March, and at five in the Afternoon arriv'd at the *Grove*, where we halted, and boiled Dumplins, of fome Flour his Ex- cellency had on one of his Horfes, which he gene-

roufly

rously diftributed to the Men. Then fetting forward, we arriv'd at Night to the afore-mention'd
Wood, near *Diego*, after fo prodigioufly fatiguing
a March, of more than twenty Miles; in which,
Numbers dropp'd down thro' the exceffive, tortur-
ing Heat, and fainting Labour, and were forc'd
to be brought up on the Horfes, which follow'd.

Friday, March 18. The Mens Feet are very
much blifter'd, and even our old Marchers jaded
to Death; and arriving on *St. Juan*'s Beach, that
hard Ground, after marching thro' the Woods,
batter'd our Feet extremely. However, we march'd
brifkly, under all thefe Difadvantages, and arriv'd
at four o' Clock to our former Camp, at *St. Wan*'s,
and again took Poffeffion of it, with Drums beating, and found the Veffels and all fafe. Juft before, arriv'd two Boats from *Frederica*, with Provifions and twenty Auxiliary *Indians* of the *Creek*
Nation, who were difpatch'd by Capt. *Mac Kay*,
and forwarded by Fort-Major *Stewart*, at *Fort-
William*. By them we were inform'd, that all was
well at *Frederica*.

Saturday, March 19. The Rangers and their
Horfes were this Morning ferry'd over to *Talbot*,
in order to proceed home; and Lieut. *Mac Kay*,
with his Highlanders, was fent in his Boat up the
Lake *de Poupa*, or *Oglethorpe*, to fee if the *Spaniards* had begun to repair the Fort of that Name,
and that of *Piccalatta*; the former of which was
kept, during the Siege of *Auguftine*, and garifon'd
by the General, firft, under Lieut. *Hugh Mac Kay*,
fince deceas'd; next under Enfign *Cathcart*, and
afterwards under Enfign *Anthony Morelon*, fince a
Lieutenant. At the Raifing the Siege, it was de-
molifhed by Capt. *Dunbar*. We boil three Days
Allowance of Beef. In the Afternoon, the afore-
faid *Indians* fet out for *St. Auguftine*, on an Expedition. Several Complaints being utter'd of the
Badnefs of the Beef and Water, his Excellency,

to

to let a good Example, eats and drinks nothing
elfe.

Sunday, March 20. Two more Boats arrive from
Frederica, with *Cherokee Indians*; and foon after a
Schooner, with the *Upper-Creeks, Cuffitaes, Ocuni's*,
and *Cowhati's*; Part of whom left us, and return'd
to *Frederica*, as before related; and fome of the *Tal-
poofes, Tuckababbe* and *Savannee* Nations, who came
to affift the General, making in all feventy. Various Conjectures are pafs'd of his Excellency's
Intentions, and the Men feem to be uneafy for
Want of Action. Our prefent Poft, if the *Spaniards* have any Souls, muft be very dangerous, and
all Precautions are taken to receive them in a
proper Manner. An *Indian* Conjurer prophefies
they will be down upon us this Night; and therefore, to humour thofe People's Superftition, a
Double-Watch is kept; and another Advanc'd-
Guard mounted under Enfign *Chamberlaine*, as far
off as the Horfe-Guards.

Monday, March 21. The *Rye* Man of War,
Capt. *Hardy*, and the *Charles-Town* Galley, Capt.
Lightfoot, on a Cruize from *Charles-Town*, and the
Succefs, Capt. *Thomfon*, appear off the Bar; and the
latter fends in his Boat for Provifions, which are
fent him; and Lieut. *Maxwell*, the General's Aid-
de-Camp, is fent in his Excellency's Cutter, to
Capt. *Hardy*, to propofe to him to cover the Landing of his Forces on the *Metanças* or *St. Anaftatia*,
where he propos'd a Defcent, to kill their Cattle,
and take their Slaves; which would, confequently,
ftarve the Town. All well in the Camp, and on
board the Veffels.

Tuefday, March 22. Mr. *Maxwell* return'd with
Capt. *Hardy's* Anfwer, which inform'd his Excellency of the Danger he imagin'd there would
be in the Attempt, and in fine, urged that he
could not pafs the Limits of the Cruize he was
upon, after a Store-Ship, which was expected
from the *Havanna*.   *Wednef-*

Wednefday, *March* 23. Lieut. *Ronald Campbell*, of the *Walker*, is fent on fome Bufinefs to Capt. *Thomfon*; and Capt. *Davis*, to Commodore *Hardy*.

The Siege of *Auguftine*, and the continual Incurfions fince made by his Excellency, having quite render'd the open Country, from *St. Mathia's* to *Auguftine*, ufelefs to the *Spaniards*, (and fpoil'd their ufual Methods of decoying our Negroes from *Carolina*, and elfewhere; whence, in Numbers, they ufed to defert to them, before the Settlement of *Georgia*, and were, on embracing their Religion, inftated in certain Lands, which they held of that Government;) they kept all their Cattle on the *Metanças* or *St. Anaftatia*, guarded by Slaves. The Deftruction of thefe would have produc'd fatal Effects to the *Spaniards*; and the Hazard of it made it one of the boldeft Attempts that has of late been heard of: For the Troops muft have been landed on a Beach, where the Sea ran Mountains high with the leaft Breath of Wind, and under the very Cannon of the Caftle, and where the Ships are every Moment in Danger of being blown from their Anchors and driven on Shore; (and tho', at the Siege of *Auguftine*, the brave Major *Alexander Heron*, fince made a Lieutenant Colonel, by Brevet, in the Abfence of Lieutenant-Colonel *William Cook*, at the Time of the late Invafion, where he fo much diftinguifh'd himfelf, landed here; yet his Boats were moftly over-fet, Numbers loft their Arms, and fome few narrowly efcap'd lofing their Lives.) What a Difappointment was the not fucceeding of this Scheme, to us all? which would have given us *Auguftine* almoft without a Siege, and perhaps had given their Galleys to us without a Blow. At four o' Clock, the *Indians*, that went on *Saturday* to *Auguftine*, return'd, having been no farther then the *Grove*, where they were repuls'd by the *Yamafees*, who, it feems, were out, and

and one of them wounded. They appear'd prodigiously jaded and fatigu'd.

Thursday, March 24. The *Rye,* and *Charles-Town* Galley return to their Cruize, Capt. *Thomson* remaining off the Bar at Anchor. The General resolves, even with what Vessels he has, to go to the *Metanças.*

Friday, March 25. Fifty *Indians* set out on another Incursion to *Augustine,* after physicking, and performing the War-Dance, with more Ceremony than I ever saw them.

Saturday, March 26. At Noon his Excellency embark'd in the *Walker,* with forty Soldiers, besides the Ship's Crew, and forty-six *Indians,* who were resolv'd to go on this Sea-Expedition with him; which was an extraordinary Offer from them, and show'd their Value for the General, whom they call their Father. Captain *Carr* was left, with his Scout-Boats, to wait for those *Indians* who went by Land. The Remainder of the Detachment embark'd in the other Boats. The rude Manners of the *Indians* on board, who without Ceremony took up the Cabin and all the Conveniencies, for Lodging, and their Arms, and Lumber, were somewhat irksome, especially considering their Nastiness; however, as his Excellency himself was pleased with lying roughly on the Deck, all the Voyage, no body else had the least Reason to complain.

Sunday, March 27. At seven A. M. we weigh with little Wind at S. S. W. and foggy. From the Sand-Hills our Course was E. S. E. over the Bar. At ten A. M. all the Fleet got over the Bar, consisting of one Ship, four Schooners, and seven smaller Vessels, as Perriaguas, &c. At Noon Captain *Thomson* bore off N. N. E. distant about three Leagues: We send his Boat with Provisions, and man our Long-Boat, to weigh an Anchor he left behind him; but the Buoy-Rope broke, and they came without it. The Wind blowing fresh at

S. W. the General order'd the fmaller Veffels to bear away to *Frederica*, inland, and the reft of us kept plying to Wind-ward. At feven P. M. we all come to an Anchor in feven Fathom Water, off *Talbot* Inlet, with little Wind at S. W. the Ship four Miles to Leeward.

Monday, March 28. At fix A. M. we all weigh'd, with the Wind at Weft, and moderate; but could not fee the *Succefs*. At eight D°, the Wind chop'd to W. N. W. At nine defcry a Sail, which we give Chace to, and clear Ship for fighting; at eleven D°, come up with her, and find her, to our Difappointment, Captain *Thomfon*, who came on board to the General, and inform'd him of the Death of his Lieutenant, Mr. *Baine*, and the Illnefs of Lieutenant *Sterling*, Officer of the Command on board. The Wind continuing at W. N. W. we all fteer in for *Auguftine* Bar, clear Weather; at three, P. M. we are clofe in with the faid Bar, where we fee two Sloops; we keep clofe along Shore, and the General, taking two of the *Indian* Chiefs, went in his Cutter to fee if he could land his Men on *Anaftatia*; but found it was not poffible, the Sea ran fo high. We defcry on the Beach one *Spaniard* on Horfeback, and two other Scouts on Foot, who fire a Mufket. We plainly open *Auguftine* Town and Caftle, which make a pretty Appearance from Sea, feeming all to be built of white Stone : We ftand clofe in with the *Metanças*, where we fee one Galley; and the Wind fhifting to N. N. W. we ftood off and on all Night with eafy Sail.

The *Indians* begin to be tired of the Sea, and want fadly to be fet on Shore; which being impoffible, his Excellency ftrives to divert their Minds, by amufing them with fuch Curiofities as he had on board, fhewing them the Nature of the Compafs, &c. at which they exprefs'd a very natural and beautiful Surprize and Amazement.   *Tuefday,*

Tuesday, March 29. This Morning being moderate, and the Wind at N. N. E. we ſtood cloſe in with the *Metanças.* At Noon the Enemy made a large Smoke, when by an accurate Obſervation we found the *Metanças-Bar* to lie in Lat. 29°. 32'. N. Wind at N. E. We ſtand to the Northward, and ſee a long Galley lying within the Bar. At four P. M. there being but little Wind at E. we got out our Oars, and clear'd Ship for fighting, the General encouraging the Rowers by handling an Oar himſelf; but Night coming on before we got the Length of the Bar, we could do nothing; only the General ſent his Cutter to ſee what was to be diſcover'd. They ſoon return'd, being able to ſee nothing but the Galley, and acquainting his Excellency, that the Eaſterly Sea ran Mountains high on Shore : So there being no Poſſibility of landing, we ſtood on and off all Night, the Wind S. E.

Wedneſday, March 30. At one A. M. we tack'd and ſtood in for the Land; at three D°, ſtood off, it inclining to be calm; at eight D°, made a Signal to ſpeak with the Maſters of the Tranſports, *Mac Kenſie, Warren,* and *Nunez* ; and we all ſtood in for *St. Auguſtine-Bar,* with little Wind at E. and hot Weather. We ſee lying within the Bar, one Galley and two Half-Galleys, who not daring to venture out, the General would have landed and attack'd them from Shore; but found it impracticable ſtill, the Sea ran ſo high: So finding it impoſſible to land, after alarming and inſulting the whole Coaſt by Sea, as he had their Caſtle by Land, he ordered to bear away for *St. Juan*'s. Little Wind at S. E. we ſet all our ſmall Sails. At five P. M. the General ſent his Aid-de-Camp on board the *Succeſs,* with Orders for her and the other Veſſels to make the beſt of their Way home. At eight D°, we came to an Anchor off *St. Juan's-*

E

Bar,

Bar, in nine Fathom Water, with the Wind at
S. E. and moderate.

Thurſday, March 31. At ſix A. M. weigh'd and
ſtood in cloſe for the Bar. At ſeven D°, his Excellency went aſhore in his Cutter; and ſoon after we
ſet the *Indians* on Shore, firing thirteen Guns as they
went over the Side. Beer was given afterwards
to our Men, and under the Diſcharge of our Cannon, we named the Mount at the Entrance of this
Bar, OGLETHORPE'S MOUNT. The *Indians* not
being return'd from *Auguſtine*, the General waits
for them; and therefore at the Return of our
Boat, we weigh'd, Wind at S. S. E. At three
P. M. we were a-breaſt of *Fort-William*, and fired
two Guns, as the Signal. At ſix D°, ſtood over
the Bar of *St. Simon*'s into the *Sound*, and found
the *Succeſs* on her Station. We proceeded direct-
ly for *Frederica*, and at nine at Night landed there;
the other Veſſels being arriv'd ſafe the Morning
paſt.

A few Days after, the General return'd with
the Remainder of his Party, and all the *Indians*;
thoſe who went to *Auguſtine*, not having taken
any Priſoner, nor ſeen a *Spaniard* without the Walls;
ſo much were they terrify'd with our late Attempts. And ſince this, ſeveral Parties of our *Indians* have been out, to their very Gates, and kept
the Watches in the utmoſt Panic and Fear,
bringing his Excellency three or four Priſoners,
at different Times, all whom he has carried to
England with him.

. When I reflect upon General *Oglethorpe*'s great
Qualities, and his indefatigable Zeal in ſerving his
Country; his many hazardous and painful Expedi-
tions (particularly that of the Siege of *Auguſtine*, in
which he was betray'd and neglected by the mean
Carolina Regiment, and many of the Men of
War;) and his late glorious Defeat of the *Spa-*
niſh

niſh Invaſion of *Georgia :* When I reflect on his
breaking a good and vigorous Conſtitution, to render the Perſons under his Command, eaſy and
happy ; his extending his Compaſſion to the Miſera-
ble of all Sorts, and in ſhort, his Poſſeſſion of every
Civil and Military Virtue ; I am ſhock'd, that
Envy itſelf dare mean to taint his Character with
its foul Blaſt: But what Merit is Proof againſt
ſome foul Tongues, and fouler Hearts ; when God
himſelf cannot eſcape them ? But he will ſoon
prove to them, that there are other Qualities than
Impudence, and a Knack at Slander, requir'd for
the Taſk of oppoſing his excellent and juſt Mea-
ſures. —— From an impartial Survey of his Actions, the Tendency of which, I have, perhaps,
had many Opportunities to contemplate, I can't
forbear to ſing with *Addiſon,* only with the Va-
riation of the Perſon,

> Oglethorpe's *Acts appear divinely bright,*
> *And proudly ſhine in their own native Light.*
> *Rais'd of themſelves, their genuine Charms they boaſt ;*
> *And thoſe who paint them trueſt, praiſe them moſt.*

I can't relinquiſh my Subject, Dear Sir, without juſt touching on the Character of a young
Gentleman, who was left Commander in Chief at
Frederica, in the General's Abſence, Captain-Lieu-
tenant *James Mackay* ; who at an early Age,
and in a Service, where the Marrow of the Military is hardly acquirable, has eſtabliſhed the Reputation of an able and experienc'd Officer: But
that Encomium, you'll find, falls far ſhort of the
reſt of his Character, when I inform you, that to
the ſweeteſt Temper, is join'd the moſt generous
Soul. Couragious, juſt, virtuous, humane, kind,
and temperate, he bleſſes all who know him, and
reſtores the Golden Age wherever he appears : And
'tis not barely Gratitude for Favours received, that
draws

draws from me this Panegyric; but the Conviction I am under, that he deferves this, and more, from all that ever had the Honour to be acquainted with him.

I conclude, Honoured Sir, with expreffing the fame Sentiments of Gratitude to a Gentleman who has been the Solace and Tutor of every Hour I have fpent in this Country, and to whom I owe all the little military Knowledge I may. or fhall be poffefs'd of. To explain whom I mean, may I be continually deferving of the Friendfhip of Lieutenant *Anthony Morelon*, (at whofe Defire this Journal was at firft undertaken;) a Gentleman as amiable and ufeful in his private Character, as he is by the Confeffion of the beft Judges acknowledged to be, in his Capacity of a good and able Officer.

I long to embrace you, to throw myfelf at your Feet; but you'll allow fome Time to the Workings of a laudable Ambition, and to the Defire I have to render myfelf worthy the Favour and Protection of fo great a Man, as General *Oglethorpe*; to deferve which, is to deferve all that's good in Life. Tho' you have loft, for a Time, your dear E——— K———r, yet you may ever expect the fame tender, requifite and due Regards from him, who; tho' in Name different, in Sentiment will always be like him; and to you, to whom I owe all I am, or poffefs in my Mind,

Ever moft dutiful, obedient, and affectionate.

G. L. CAMPBELL,
v. E. K.

INDEXES.

Index to the introduction

www.ingramcontent.com/pod-product-compliance
Lightning Source LLC
Chambersburg PA
CBHW031538040426
42445CB00010B/598